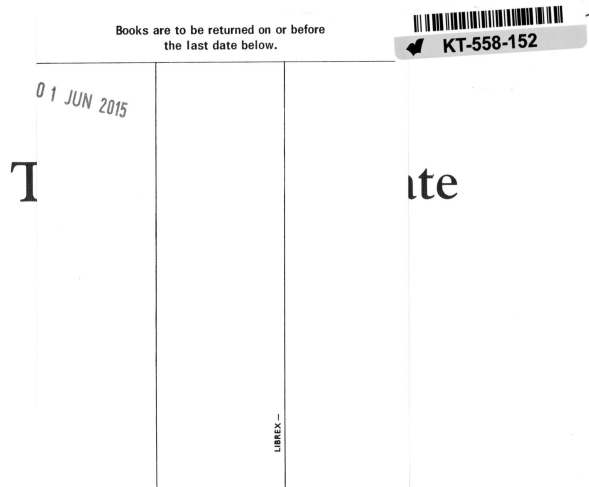

T ate

Volume 63

Editor

Craig Donnellan

Independence

Educational Publishers

First published by Independence
PO Box 295
Cambridge CB1 3XP
England

British Library Cataloguing in Publication Data
The Racism Debate – (Issues Series)
I. Donnellan, Craig II. Series
305.8'00941

ISBN 1 86168 239 5

Printed in Great Britain
MWL Print Group Ltd

Typeset by
Claire Boyd

Cover
The illustration on the front cover is by
Pumpkin House.

CONTENTS

Chapter One: Racial Discrimination

Chapter Two: Tackling Racism

Introduction

The Racism Debate is the sixty-third volume in the **Issues** series. The aim of this series is to offer up-to-date information about important issues in our world.

The Racism Debate examines racial discrimination and ways to tackle it.

The information comes from a wide variety of sources and includes:
Government reports and statistics
Newspaper reports and features
Magazine articles and surveys
Web site material
Literature from lobby groups
and charitable organisations.

It is hoped that, as you read about the many aspects of the issues explored in this book, you will critically evaluate the information presented. It is important that you decide whether you are being presented with facts or opinions. Does the writer give a biased or an unbiased report? If an opinion is being expressed, do you agree with the writer?

The Racism Debate offers a useful starting-point for those who need convenient access to information about the many issues involved. However, it is only a starting-point. At the back of the book is a list of organisations which you may want to contact for further information.

*****

Racism

What is racism?

Racism is treating someone differently or unfairly simply because they belong to a different race or culture.

People can also experience prejudice because of their religion or nationality.

Racism takes many different forms. These can include:

- Personal attacks of any kind, including violence
- Written or verbal threats or insults
- Damage to property, including graffiti.

Why are people racist?

Unfortunately racism can exist in all races and cultures. Racists feel threatened by anyone who is from a different race or culture.

We are not born racist. Our views and beliefs develop as we grow up. If a child or young person grows up within a racist family, or has friends who are racist, they may believe that racism is normal and acceptable.

Prejudice of any kind is often based on ignorance and fear of anything unfamiliar.

The law

The Race Relations (Amendment) Act 2000 strengthens the Race Relations Act 1976 in Great Britain, which makes it illegal to discriminate in the fields of employment, education, housing, and the provision of goods, services and facilities. In addition to this, the amendment also extends to the Public Sector. The Race Relations Order 1997, which applies to Northern Ireland, covers the same issues.

Both these UK Government Acts give people the right to bring their complaint before an employment tribunal or a court. Racist incidents ranging from harassment and abuse to physical violence are offences under the criminal law. Inciting racial hatred is also a criminal offence. Racially offensive material in the media contravenes media codes of practice. Complaints can be made to the Press Complaints Commission or the Broadcasting Standards Authority.

The effects of racism

If a young person is experiencing racism of any kind, they may become lonely and sad. They may also try to avoid situations where racist behaviour could occur, and pretend to be ill, play truant from school, or be scared to leave their house.

Challenging racism

All racist acts are unacceptable. The Government has put anti-racist laws into place to protect all members of the community. In many schools young people and teachers work together to produce anti-bullying policies, which include sections on racist bullying. Many companies, when advertising for jobs, try to attract applications from all ethnic minorities as well as all other sections of the community. This is called 'equal opportunities', and enables everyone who is applying for a job to have the same chance of securing a job, regardless of their race, culture, age, religion, colour, marital status, gender, sexuality or disability.

What children have told ChildLine

In 2000/2001 ChildLine received 525 calls and letters from children about racist bullying, and a further 47 calls and letters from children who had encountered other forms of racism.

Children and Racism, a study into calls and letters to ChildLine, was published in 1997. When children and young people contacted ChildLine about racism, they spoke of their sadness, anger, hurt and dismay.

This is what some children told ChildLine:

- Sharon, 16, is dating a Pakistani boy. Her parents are racist, so she has to keep her relationship a secret, which is making her feel anxious.

- Sandra, 11, is called racist names as she is black. She is scared to tell her teacher, in case the bullying gets worse.
- Ravinder, 15, is being beaten up by a group of boys at school, because he is Asian.
- Alice, 9, is being bullied at school, as she is the only white girl in her class.
- Clive, 13, has just moved to Scotland from England. A gang of Scottish boys at school calls him names.
- Sunitta, 14, is being called racist names at school. Racist comments are also written about her on the wall of the toilets. Her teacher hasn't done anything about it.
- Dina, 12, is teased because she is Italian. She has to have extra lessons for her English reading and writing. She feels nervous about going to school.

Unfortunately racism can exist in all races and cultures. Racists feel threatened by anyone who is from a different race or culture

---

How ChildLine can help

ChildLine takes children's and young people's problems seriously, giving them a chance to talk in confidence about their concerns or worries, however large or small. ChildLine counsellors can also put young people in touch with helpful adults and further information, including local sources of help and advice. ChildLine is free and available 24 hours a day, seven days a week.

ChildLine
Freephone: 0800 1111 or FREEPOST 1111, London N1 0BR or ChildLine Minicom: 0800 400 222. Mon-Fri 9.30am-9.30pm. Sat-Sun 9.30am-8.00pm. Web site: www.childline.org.uk

Other sources of help

Commission for Racial Equality, Elliot House, 10-12 Allington Street, London SW1E 5EH. Tel: 020 7932 5281. Web site: www.cre.org.uk

Equal Opportunities Commission, Overseas House, Quay Street, Manchester M3 3HN. Tel: 0161 833 9244. Web site: www.eoc.org.uk

Equality Commission Northern Ireland, Andras House, 60 Great Victoria Street, Belfast BT2 7BB. Tel: 02890 500600. Web site: www.equalityni.org

© *ChildLine January 2002*

Multi-cultural United Kingdom

The UK today has a richly diverse society and culture which date back thousands of years. African divisions of Roman soldiers were stationed at Hadrian's Wall in the third century. Even the patron saint of England, St George, was not English and lived and died in the Middle East.

After the battle of Hastings in 1066 French culture was added to the Anglo-Saxon and Celtic cultures already existing in our islands. At the same time the first Jewish community was being developed in the UK. By the sixteenth century gypsies arrived on our shores and by the mid-eighteenth century there was a black community, mainly in London, of 15,000.

Throughout the centuries the UK has always welcomed people from different parts of the world who were being persecuted. After the Second World War the UK invited Blacks and Asians to help reconstruct a battered country.

Today the UK has a minority ethnic population of more than 3 million people (about six per cent of the population). This ethnic diversity has enriched the UK and has contributed to its economic, social, democratic and cultural development.

In sports ethnic minorities have gained a third of all Olympic medals won by the UK since 1984. Gold medal winners include Daley Thompson, Tessa Sanderson, Linford Christie, Denise Lewis and Audley Harrison.

Forty-two per cent of the British world athletics championship squad and sixteen per cent of professional footballers in England and Wales were from the ethnic minority population. As well as this the English national cricket and football teams have been captained and our four greatest boxers in the last seventy years have come from the ethnic minority population.

In the world of literature six UK ethnic minority authors have been nominated for the Booker Prize. Great UK authors like V.S. Naipaul, Hanif Kureishi and Arundhati Roy have enriched our literature lives.

Bill Morris, General Secretary of the Transport and General Workers' Union, one of the UK's largest trade unions' has protected and bettered millions of workers' employment terms and conditions. In the professional field of health a tenth of all hospital staff are of Indian ethnicity and are the mainstays of specialist areas including psychiatry and geriatric medicine.

Our national dish is Indian curry and 2.5 million curries are eaten per week in the UK. This has created a £2 billion-a-year industry which employs more people in the UK than the combined totals of the coal, steel and ship-building industries.

A recent report warns that Britons will have to work until their seventies unless more immigration is encouraged.
- The above information is from Race for Racial Justice's web site : www.racialjustice.org.uk

© *Race for Racial Justice*

Replacing myths with facts

2001 census

The Commission for Racial Equality (CRE) today welcomed the results of the 2001 census.

Beverley Bernard, Acting Chair of the CRE, said: 'This data not only helps us substitute myths with facts, it also provides a benchmark from which to accurately assess the impact of measures to improve race relations.

'The extent of diversity shown by the census is balanced by other recent research, which shows we are also a society united by common interests.'

A recent MORI poll found that people estimated that ethnic minorities comprised 22.5% of the total population, nearly three times the actual size

---

The figures released today reveal that many commentators have overestimated the size of the ethnic minority population. A recent MORI poll found that people estimated that ethnic minorities comprised 22.5% of the total population, nearly three times the actual size.

'We look forward to the publication of more detailed data in the coming months which will provide

---

information on age, education, and health among other factors – all vital to determining equality of opportunity and equality of access to goods and services.'

The CRE is pleased to note the inclusion of data on religious groups, as it is an important factor in self-definition and identity, particularly among ethnic minority groups. While Britain remains an overwhelmingly Christian country – with nearly three-quarters of the population classifying itself as Christian – significant minorities include 3% who are Muslim, 1.1% Hindu, 0.6% Sikh, and 0.5% Jewish.

For the first time, the census includes data on Britain's mixed race population, that stands at nearly 1.4%. It also includes data on the number of Irish in England and Wales, which is 1.2% of the population.

Ms Bernard said: 'It is important to recognise that both these groups suffer discrimination and disadvantage in education, health, and housing. They are also overrepresented in social care.

'The release of this data provides fascinating new insights into Britain's multiracial society. It will be an invaluable resource for the public, private, and voluntary sectors both in setting employment targets and ensuring equal access to goods and services over the next ten years.'

■ The above information is from the Commission for Racial Equality's web site: www.cre.gov.uk

© *Commission for Racial Equality*

Race definitions

Information from Race for Racial Justice

Racism: a set of attitudes and behaviour towards another racial or ethnic group based on:

- The belief that natural difference in physical characteristics (such as skin colour, hair type, face shape, etc.) corresponds directly to differences in personality and ability.
- The social and economic power of members of one racial or ethnic group to enforce and enact such attitudes and behaviour towards others.

Institutional racism
Procedures, practices and behaviour within an organisation or institution, which support and encourage direct or indirect racial discrimination.

Prejudice
Prejudging people in a negative way according to preconceived ideas about them.

Stereotyping
Making broad generalisations about particular groups of people and expecting all members of that group to think and behave identically.

Positive discrimination
Treating people more favourably on the grounds of race, nationality, religion, gender etc. (Under the Race Relations Act this is illegal in the UK.)

Positive action
Offering special help to people who are disadvantaged because of prejudice, stereotyping and discrimination, in order that they may take full and equal advantage of opportunities in jobs, education, training, services, etc.

Affirmative action
A term commonly used in the USA to refer to positive discrimination.

Direct discrimination
Treating people less favourably because of race, nationality, religion, gender, etc.

Indirect discrimination
Applying a rule or requirement, which effectively leads to less favourable conditions or treatment for a particular group of people.

Ethnicity
A sense of cultural and historical identity based on belonging by birth to a distinctive cultural group.

Stereotyping is making broad generalisations about particular groups of people

---

Ethnocentricity
Viewing the world from the perspective of one particular ethnic group, often with the assumption that the values, beliefs and achievements of that group are superior to those of other ethnic groups.

Nationalism
A distinctive sense of cultural and historical identity or common destiny based on being a citizen of a particular nation state.

Multi-culturalism
The belief that many different cultures should be encouraged and allowed to flourish in society and that services and facilities such as health, education, the arts, etc. should be delivered in a way that embodies and promotes this belief.

- The above information is from Race for Racial Justice's web site which can be found at www.racialjustice.org.uk Alternatively see page 41 for their postal address details.

© Race for Racial Justice

Prejudice is pre-judging people in a negative way according to preconceived ideas about them

---

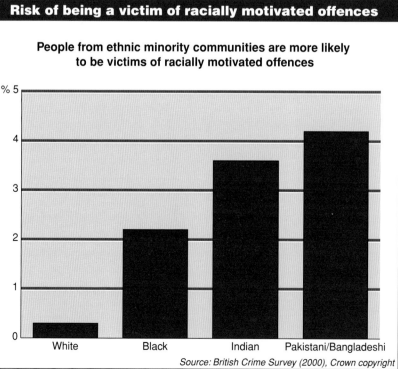

Risk of being a victim of racially motivated offences

People from ethnic minority communities are more likely to be victims of racially motivated offences

Source: British Crime Survey (2000), Crown copyright

We live in a racist society, reveals ICM poll

More than half of Britons have someone from a different ethnic background in their immediate circle of friends

More than half of the British population believe they live in a racist society, according to a major survey on race relations.

But more than half of Britons have someone from a different ethnic background in their immediate circle of friends.

The opinion poll commissioned by BBC News Online also found that 44% of those asked believe immigration has damaged Britain over the last 50 years. But the ICM study goes on to suggest that most whites, blacks and Asians agree society is more racially tolerant than a decade ago.

The survey, part of a major BBC News Online series on race relations in the UK, also indicates widespread support for plans to introduce citizenship classes and English lessons for people applying to live in the UK.

Between 7 and 11 May, ICM Research interviewed 1,576 people aged 18 and over. The interviews were conducted face to face and quotas were used to ensure that at least 500 interviews were conducted with people from white, black and Asian backgrounds.

The data collected was then weighted to bring it into a balance with a national profile of all adults. The margin of error for the poll is plus or minus 3%.

However, this margin increases when the answers are based on smaller groups within the total sample. For example, when just Asian people are mentioned or when other individual groups are extracted from the total number of people asked.

The survey reveals that racism in the workplace is a major problem – with almost one in three blacks and Asians saying they believe racism has cost them the chance of a job.

But it also suggests widespread acceptance of mixed-race relation-

ships. Half of all those asked say they would marry or have a relationship with someone from another race.

Tolerant

And when asked how they would feel if their child married someone from another race, most said the most important thing would be that they had found a loving partner.

The opinion poll, weighted to include the views of whites, blacks and Asians in the UK, is one of the largest surveys on race conducted in recent years.

More than half of each group said they feel that Britain is now more tolerant racially than it was 10 years ago.

But of all those questioned, 51% said they felt Britain is a racist society.

Of all those questioned, 51% said they felt Britain is a racist society. That view was shared by 52% of whites and 53% of blacks

---

That view was shared by 52% of whites and 53% of blacks.

Among Asian respondents, 41% said they believe Britain is racist compared with 45% who rejected the suggestion.

Contribution

Meanwhile, 47% of whites said they felt immigration had harmed society in the last 50 years, compared with 28% who felt it had benefited Britain.

And almost two-thirds of whites said they believe immigrants do not integrate or make a positive contribution to Britain.

On the idea of English lessons and citizenship classes for 'anyone not familiar with the British way of life and living full-time in the UK', 78% of all those asked agreed with the proposals.

On employment, 40% of blacks and 34% of Asians said they have come across racism at work.

■ The above information is from the Black Information Link's web site which can be found at www.blink.org.uk

© *Black Information Link/The 1990 Trust*

Minority ethnic groups in the UK

Astatistical picture of minority ethnic groups in the United Kingdom is drawn by a new report from the Office for National Statistics. Published today* on the National Statistics web site only, it looks at the characteristics and circumstances of the UK's minority ethnic groups.

The data in this report are drawn from Annual Local Area Labour Force Survey, British Crime Survey, Family Resources Survey, Health Survey for England, Labour Force Survey and the Youth Cohort Study. 2001 Census results estimating the numbers and demographic characteristics and geographical spread of the minority ethnic population will be published starting February 2003. This report will be updated with these data when available.

Population

- The size of the minority ethnic population was 4.5 million in 2001/02 or 7.6 per cent of the total population of the United Kingdom. Indians were the largest minority group, followed by Pakistanis, Black Caribbeans, Black Africans, and those of Mixed ethnic backgrounds.
- Minority ethnic groups have a younger age structure than the White population. In 2001/02 the Mixed group had the youngest age structure – more than half (55 per cent) were under the age of 16. The White group had the highest proportion of people aged 65 and over at 16 per cent.

The minority ethnic population was 4.5 million in 2001/02 or 7.6 per cent of the total population of the United Kingdom

- In England people from minority ethnic groups made up 9 per cent of the total population in 2001/02 compared with only 2 per cent in both Scotland and Wales. Nearly half (48 per cent) of the total minority ethnic population lived in the London region, where they comprised 29 per cent of all residents.
- Asian households tend to be larger than those from other ethnic groups. In spring 2002, Bangladeshi households were the largest with an average of 4.7 people, followed by Pakistanis (4.2 people), and Indians (3.3 people).
- In spring 2002, the proportion of lone-parent families was highest among the Mixed group, at 61

In England people from minority ethnic groups made up 9 per cent of the total population in 2001/ 2002 compared with only 2 per cent in both Scotland and Wales

per cent of all families with dependent children, followed by Black Caribbeans (54 per cent).

Labour market

- People in minority ethnic groups in the UK had higher unemployment rates than White

Minority ethnic groups

In 2001, a national survey called the Census was carried out of the whole population in Britain. This has the most recent and accurate figures possible on the number of people from different ethnic groups. 92.15% of the population of Britain (more than nine out of every ten people) gave their ethnic group as white British. This was higher in the North-East, Wales and the South-West, where over 95% described themselves as white British. Taking England separately, the percentage of people from minority ethnic groups has grown from 6% to 9% since 1991. Someone's ethnic group is not the same as where they were born. 87.4% of people in England (and 97% of people living in Wales) were born in Britain.

Group	% of UK population	Other details and notes
White	92.1%	
Indian	0.5%	Indians make up 25.7% of Leicester's population.
Bangladeshi	0.5%	The London borough of Tower Hamlets has the highest proportion of Bangladeshis in England and Wales.
Pakistani	1.3%	Over half of Pakistanis live in the West Midlands, Yorkshire and the North West.
Other Asian	0.4%	Thais, Sri Lankans, Malaysians etc.
Black Caribbean	1%	Black Caribbeans form 10% of the population of the London boroughs of Lewisham, Lambeth Brent and Hackney.
Black African	0.8%	About 10% of Southwark, Newham, Lambeth and Hackney are Black African.
Other Black	0.2%	About 2% of people describe themselves as Other Black in Hackey, Lambeth and Lewisham.
Chinese	0.4%	Chinese people form just over 2% of the population in Cambridge, Westminster, Barnet and in the City of London.
Mixed	1.2%	The largest proportions of peole of mixed origin are in London, with the exception of Nottingham, where 2% of people are Mixed White and Black Caribbean. This group has grown since the 1991 census.
Other	0.4%	

Source: Britkid

people in 2001/02. Bangladeshi men and women had the highest unemployment rates at 20 per cent and 24 per cent respectively.

- In 2001/02 just over 40 per cent of Bangladeshi men aged under 25 were unemployed compared with 12 per cent of young White men.
- People from Pakistani and Chinese groups are far more likely to be self-employed than those in other groups. Around one-fifth of Pakistani (22 per cent) and Chinese (19 per cent) people in employment were self-employed in 2001/02. This compares with only one in ten White people and less than one in ten Black people.

Income

- In 2000/01 Pakistani and Bangladeshi households in Great Britain were more reliant than other groups on social security benefits – which made up nearly a fifth (19 per cent) of their gross income. Benefits were also a considerable source of income for the Black group (15 per cent).
- In 2000/01 people from minority ethnic groups were more likely than White people to live in low-income households in Great Britain. Almost 60 per cent of the Pakistani/Bangladeshi group were living in low-income households before housing costs were deducted. This increased to 68 per cent after housing costs.

Education

- Indian girls and boys in England and Wales were more likely to get five or more GCSEs at grades A*-C than their White, Black, Pakistani and Bangladeshi counterparts. Sixty-six per cent of Indian girls and 54 per cent of Indian boys achieved this in 1999.
- In 2001/02, people from Chinese, Indian, Black African and Other Asian groups were more likely to have degrees than White people in the UK. Pakistanis and Bangladeshis were the most likely to be unqualified.

Victims of crime

- In 1999 in England and Wales

the risk of being the victim of a racially motivated incident was considerably higher for members of minority ethnic groups than for White people. The highest risk was for Pakistani and Bangladeshi people at 4.2 per cent, followed by 3.6 per cent for Indian people and 2.2 per cent for Black people. This compared with 0.3 per cent for White people.

Health

- In England, Asians were considerably more likely than the general population to describe their health as bad or very bad in 1999. After standardising for age, Pakistani/Bangladeshi men and women were three to four times more likely than the general population to rate their health in this way.
- In 1999 Bangladeshi men and women living in England were nearly six times more likely than the general population to report having diabetes after standardising for age. Risk ratios among Pakistani men and women were almost as high as those for the Bangladeshi group. Indian men and women were almost three times as likely as the general population to report having diabetes.

Lifestyles

- In England in 1999, Bangladeshi men were the group most likely to smoke cigarettes (44 per cent), followed by Irish (39 per cent) and Black Caribbean men (35 per cent). Among women, Irish and Black Caribbeans had the highest cigarette smoking rates, although only Irish women (33 per cent) had rates higher than the general population (27 per cent).
- In England in 1999, more than 34 per cent of Irish men and almost a fifth of Irish women drank above 21 units of alcohol a

week for men and 14 units a week for women. All other minority ethnic groups were less likely than the general population to drink above these levels.

Background notes

1. The Annual Local Area Labour Force Survey data presented here have been weighted to be consistent with the best population estimates available before the results of the 2001 Census were published. New regional and local mid-year population estimates for 1992-2000, which are consistent with the 2001 Census figures, will be published by ONS in early spring 2003. When these data are available, a reweighting of all the Labour Force Survey (LFS) series will be carried out. This will be complete in autumn 2003. The data presented here will then be replaced by final estimates which are consistent with the new population estimates derived from 2001 Census.
2. Details of the policy governing the release of new data are available from the press office.
3. National Statistics are produced to high professional standards set out in the National Statistics Code of Practice. They undergo regular quality assurance reviews to ensure that they meet customer needs. They are produced free from any political interference.

* Social Focus in Brief: Ethnicity, 2002. Internet-only publication. Available free on the National Statistics web site: www.statistics.gov.uk/statbase/ Product.asp?vlnk=9763

Survey on race

Summary of main findings

Careers

- 2 in 3 women think race can limit either a person's choice of career or career progression.
- More non-whites think race can limit a person's career progression than whites (75% vs 66%)
- 3 in 4 are against positive discrimination at work in terms of sex, race or age.
- 1 in 3 are in favour of positive discrimination in the police, while 1 in 4 women are in favour of positive discrimination in all other fields.
- Non-whites are more likely to be in favour of positive discrimination in police, politics or education.
- Nearly all women think health professions offer the most opportunities to ethnic minorities.
- 2 in 3 think teaching or media offer the most opportunities to ethnic minorities.
- Half of women think law or the police offer the most opportunities to ethnic minorities.
- White women are more likely to think health, media, law, police and armed forces all offer opportunities than non-white women.
- Half of women think Britain is an equal opportunity society.

Role models

- The positions of Prime Minister, the Head of MI5 or the Chief of Defence Staff were considered the most likely never to be occupied by someone from an ethnic minority.
- The positions of the Editor of the *Sun* and the English/Scottish/Irish/Welsh Football Manager were all considered most likely to be filled by someone from an ethnic minority by 2010.
- Labour is seen as the first party most likely to have an ethnic minority leader.
- 1 in 20 women think the Conservatives will be the first party to have an ethnic minority leader.

Children

- 2 in 3 women think children from different ethnic minorities are being integrated into society.
- More non-whites think children from different ethnic minorities are being integrated into society.
- Culture is the main reason children are not being integrated into society, which is ranked marginally higher than prejudice.
- 1 in 4 women think prejudice is the main reason children are not being integrated into society.
- 1 in 4 women think schools in Britain always encourage racial integration.
- 2 in 3 women think schools in Britain sometimes encourage racial integration.
- 1 in 20 women think schools never encourage racial integration.
- White women are more likely to think schools always encourage racial integration than non-white women.

Relationships

- 1 in 5 women do not have any friends from different racial backgrounds.
- 3 in 5 women have a few friends from different racial backgrounds.
- 1 in 5 women have many friends from different racial backgrounds.
- Over half of non-white women claim they have many friends from different racial backgrounds compared to one in seven white women.

- 3 in 4 women think mixed race relationships are a good thing
- 1 in 3 women think it is better to go out with someone the same race as you.
- 1 in 4 women would never have a mixed race relationship.
- 1 in 3 women say their family would disapprove if they had a mixed race relationship.
- Over 4 in 5 women think mixed race relationships enhance understanding of different cultures.

Methodology

- An omnibus survey was conducted by telephone for *She* magazine and the Commission for Racial Equality.
- The report is based on 1133 analysed questionnaires which were conducted by telephone between 2 and 17 February 2002.
- The sample is nationally representative of women aged 16+ years, and also includes a boost sample of 100 women from ethnic minorities.
- Unless specifically stated, there was no significant difference in response from ethnic minority and others.
- Data processing and computer tabulation of the results was undertaken by BMRB International.

- This report was compiled by the research team of the National Magazine Company

© *CRE/She Magazine*

Minorities accuse TV and radio of tokenism

By Helen Carter

Audiences from minority ethnic groups complained about tokenism, negative stereotyping and simplistic portrayal of their communities on television in a report published yesterday.

But programmes such as the comedy shows *Goodness Gracious Me* and *Ali G* and the long-running soap *Coronation Street* were praised as being steps in the right direction.

The report, *Multicultural Broadcasting: Concept and Reality*, was released by the BBC, Broadcasting Standards Commission, the ITC and the Radio Authority. It explores attitudes towards multicultural broadcasting from the perspective of the audience and from within the television, radio and advertising industries.

> ## The perspectives of ethnic and racial minorities were not featured sufficiently on terrestrial television, according to 69% of those working in television

All those questioned from minority ethnic groups said their country of origin was not represented at all or was negatively portrayed on television. There was also a sense that there was not enough coverage of events concerning their countries of origin.

The perspectives of ethnic and racial minorities were not featured sufficiently on terrestrial television, according to 69% of those working in television. Of the radio sample, 45% agreed.

There was concern about stereotypical portrayal of certain issues. Groups from the Asian subcontinent spoke of the way in which arranged marriages were presented on television. They felt treatment of the issue was neither accurate nor reflective of the way in which the system has changed.

The issue of tokenism was also significant – some people felt characters from minority ethnic groups were included in programmes because it was expected they should be, resulting in characters who were ill-drawn and unimportant.

Audiences felt broadcasters had a social duty to include authentic and fair representations of minorities as it would foster understanding of different cultures and allow children to see themselves represented positively.

It was seen as important that minority groups should be included in soap operas or game shows, as they have high viewing figures. They should also be more represented as presenters in news and documentary programming.

Audiences from the subcontinent said they did not want to be labelled Asian and called for their distinctive cultural identities to be acknowledged. Similarly, those within mixed-race black groups said their issues were rarely represented.

Throughout the audience research there was an underlying feeling that as all people paid a licence fee for the BBC, it had a greater obligation to accommodate minority tastes.

Younger white participants tended to feel it was divisive to have programmes aimed at particular communities and it would be better to concentrate on achieving fairer representation in the mainstream.

Both audience and industry groups agreed that although progress has been made in the last five years, there still needs to be better representation of minorities on screen and behind the scenes.

> The issue of tokenism was also significant – some people felt characters from minority ethnic groups were included in programmes because it was expected they should be

It is apparent in the report that ethnic minority groups are still under-represented in employment. Only 32% of people in radio and 22% of those in TV agreed that numbers of people from minorities in decision-making roles had increased in the last five years.

But the overwhelming feeling among those working in the advertising industry was that commercial objectives should take priority.

Paul Bolt, director of the BSC, said: 'The report shows where things are now and what can be done in developing future policies.'

Weakness in numbers

- The number of people from minority ethnic groups on air has increased
- Only 32% of the TV industry sample thought there had been a growth in programming relevant to the groups. In radio the figure was 63%
- Only 32% of those working in radio and 22% in television agreed the number of ethnic minority staff in decision-making roles had increased in the last five years
- The perspectives of ethnic and racial minorities were not featured sufficiently on terrestrial TV, according to 69% of those in television. Of the radio sample, 45% agreed this was true

Race is no barrier to 'being British'

But there is no consistent sense of 'Britishness'

The majority of people in Britain appear to have embraced a sense of multiculturalism, with almost nine in 10 saying that being British is not about being white. But whilst 86% of the British public disagree that to be truly British you have to be white, there is no consistent view on what it means to be British.

When asked what comes to mind when thinking about the 'British way of life' people highlight attitudes and behaviour (cultural diversity 9% and people being polite 6%) rather than demographic characteristics such as ethnicity. However, more than a quarter (28%) are unable to give an answer.

The preliminary report *The Voice of Britain* is released today

> **Whilst 86% of the British public disagree that to be truly British you have to be white, there is no consistent view on what it means to be British**

(Thursday) to mark the 25th anniversary of the Commission for Racial Equality at a conference at the Royal Society of Arts. The research shows there is a common recognition that Britain is multicultural. The majority (59%) agree that Britain is a place that has good race relations between different types of people such as those from different ethnic minorities. This figure rises to 67% among ethnic minority groups.

There is also widespread respect for diversity in Britain, with four in five (78%) agreeing that it is important to respect the rights of minority groups and over half (57%) saying people should do more to learn about the systems and culture of the ethnic groups in this country, although one in four disagree (27%).

There is also a rough consensus among all ethnic groups on the rights and responsibilities of those who migrate to the UK. More than two-thirds (69%) of the GB population, and half (51%) of ethnic minority people, think ethnic minorities need to demonstrate a real commitment before they can be considered British. Three-quarters of both white (77%) and ethnic minority communities (76%) believe immigrants who do

> **There is also widespread respect for diversity in Britain, with four in five (78%) agreeing that it is important to respect the rights of minority groups**

not speak English should be made to learn it.

The research shows that people of all ethnicities massively over-estimate how many people in Britain are from an ethnic minority. Most think it is one in five (20-23%) whereas, in reality, it is only one person in 12 (7%). The proportion of the British population who are immigrants to this country is also hugely overestimated.

Kully Kaur-Ballagan, head of Ethnic Minority Research for the MORI Social Research Institute, says: 'These are encouraging results. Britain is confident about its multiculturalism. And as the findings show there is no consistent or homogeneous sense of Britishness.'

© 2002 MORI

Education

Education and racism

Education is seen by many minority ethnic families as the route out of deprivation and discrimination for their children. But, despite this high premium put on education, some groups seem to fare worse than others. When postwar immigrants first came here, there was clear evidence of discriminatory practices (such as the bussing of Asian children or the relegation of West Indian children to schools for the subnormal) which marginalised and segregated children – setting them up for failure. Today, overt racism is rare in schooling. But research suggests that other factors such as teacher expectations and possible job opportunities may have much to do with success or failure. For example, in one study of a local education authority over time, Black Caribbean pupils entered schooling as the highest achieving ethnic group but left as the group least likely to attain 5 A*-C GCSEs.

Exclusions

Low expectations and/or racial stereotyping may also be at play when it comes to the exclusion of pupils from school. Black pupils, particularly boys, are more likely to be excluded from school temporarily or permanently and exclusions now take place from primary as well as secondary schools. According to government figures for 2000/01, Black Caribbean and Black Other pupils were three times more likely than white ones to be permanently excluded from school. Whereas 13 in every 10,000 white pupils were excluded, 38 in every 10,000 Black Caribbean pupils were. The lowest rate of exclusions was for Indian pupils (3 in every 10,000).

Achievement

When it comes to achievement at school, there is quite a wide discrepancy between the way students in each group fare. Overall in 2002, Chinese pupils were most likely to get 5 or more GCSEs (grade A*-C) and Black Caribbean pupils the least likely. And girls in all ethnic groups did better than boys.

Employment and education

Young people from minority ethnic backgrounds are more likely to continue in full-time education after 16 and to get good results. 71% of minority ethnic 16- 19-year-olds are in full-time education compared with 58% of whites of the same age. Though they are 9% of the 18-24 age group, minority ethnic young people form 13% of university undergraduates.

Chinese, Indians and Black Africans are more likely than white people to have degrees or their equivalent. Yet graduate unemploy-

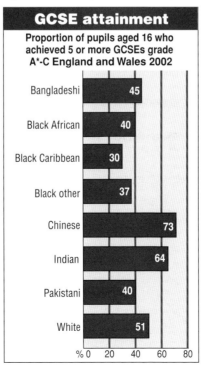

GCSE attainment

Proportion of pupils aged 16 who achieved 5 or more GCSEs grade A*-C England and Wales 2002

Group	%
Bangladeshi	45
Black African	40
Black Caribbean	30
Black other	37
Chinese	73
Indian	64
Pakistani	40
White	51

ment is much higher among minorities: 12% of African-Caribbean and 6% of Asian graduates as opposed to 3% of whites. According to the Higher Education Funding Council for England, nearly 18% of black and Asian 1995 graduates were unemployed six months after graduating – almost twice as many as their white counterparts. Even within educational institutions, there is evidence of discrimination. Figures from the Higher Education Statistics Agency (January 2002) show that, although 6.5% of all academics are classified as 'non-white', only 2%, 208 out of 11,000, professors in this country are black or Asian.

Refugee education

It is estimated that there are now around 70,000 asylum-seeker or refugee children in the UK and of these over half are in schools in London and the south-east. Obviously, such children, who have had to move very suddenly from traumatic situations, may be coming to school with particular problems and English will almost certainly not be their first language. Some children have had to flee to the UK without their family or any adults whom they know. These 'unaccompanied minors', who are estimated to be at least 6,000 in number, face severe problems and need special care. Sadly, there is even less support for refugee children than was made available for minority ethnic children in previous decades. Help with extra English classes and additional teachers for areas with many refugee children are being removed. One of the only specialist units for refugee education, in Newham (which takes the most refugees in the UK), was closed down in 2002. It has also been decided that the children in asylum-seeking families who are being held in detention centres will not join other children in normal schools in the vicinity. They will be educated in prison.

Separate schools

Because certain minority ethnic groups see that mainstream schools are failing their children, one response has been to set up separate schools to serve that particular group. For example, in 1980, a Seventh Day Adventist Christian school to serve Black Caribbean children was set up in North London. More recently, a small number of Muslim schools have been set up. (There are already separate Catholic, Protestant and Jewish schools in the UK – the law allows for any religious denomination to set up their own school.) Some groups are trying to pressure the government to give more money towards the setting up of separate schools.

However, evidence emerging from research carried out in the

Young people from minority ethnic backgrounds are more likely to continue in full-time education after 16 and to get good results

---

north-west of England following riots there in 2001, suggests that the reason for the disquiet and rioting was the division between the Asian and white communities. And the fact that young people had rarely been educated together, because of an informal segregation (separation), was a crucial factor. We believe that instead of financing more separate, religious schools (exclusive to one particular group) efforts should be made to allow all children to attend the local schools of their choice and funds given to improve services and support in those schools.

Sources: *Permanent Exclusions from Schools and Exclusion Appeals,* England 200/2001, Department for Education and Skills 2002; *Annual Labour Force Survey 2001/2; Access to what: analysis of factors determining graduate employability,* Higher Education Funding Council for England, 2002.

■ The above information is from the Institute of Race Relations' web site which can be found at www.irr.org.uk

© Institute of Race Relations 2003

Minority ethnic pupils in mainly white schools

Key findings

■ A survey of the performance of over 34,000 pupils in mainly white schools in 35 LEAs indicated that children from a White background in mainly white schools outperformed those in urban multi-ethnic schools in Key Stage 2 SATs and GCSE exams – presumably because these schools were in socially more advantaged areas.

■ Children from Black Caribbean, Indian and Pakistani backgrounds in the same schools also outperformed their urban counterparts at GCSE level but *not* at the end of Key Stage 2. Children from minority ethnic backgrounds shared in whatever educational advantages were available in these schools to the same degree as children from a White background in secondary school but not in primary school.

■ In many schools and LEAs this data was either not available or unreliable, mainly because of uncertainties around the recording of pupils' ethnic background.

■ Individual interviews in fourteen

mainly white schools indicated that aspects of ethnicity were central in the pupils' self-identification. But there was considerable variation in how far they would have liked to see their ethnic identity expressed more fully and openly at school. Schools face a challenging task in attempting to respect this range of views.

■ A significant proportion of the minority ethnic pupils reported race-related name calling or verbal abuse at school or while travelling to and from school. For example, in the questionnaire survey 26% said that they had had such experiences during the previous week.

■ No school in this sample had a fully developed strategy for preparing pupils through the curriculum for life in a diverse society. Presented with alternative ideals of how diversity might be treated, most informants saw their school or class as trying to treat all children equally and playing down ethnic and cultural differences. A minority of schools

or classrooms in this sample were seen as partially adopting the alternative stance of stressing and valuing cultural diversity.

■ Teaching provision for children in the early stages of learning English as an additional language (EAL) was variable, and no school had a strategy in place for supporting children with EAL beyond the initial stages.

■ Teachers reported that, in most cases, the issues with which this research was concerned had not been covered either in their initial training or in any recent in-service training.

By Tony Cline, Guida de Abreu, Cornelius Fihosy, Hilary Gray, Hannah Lambert and Jo Neale, University of Luton

Further information

Copies of this Research Brief (RB365) are available free of charge from tel: 0845 60 222 60. Research Briefs and Research Reports can be accessed at www.dfes.gov.uk/research

© Crown copyright

Racial violence

Every day on the streets of the UK, in playgrounds, classrooms, shops, at work, minority ethnic people are racially harassed

This can take any form, from a racist remark to a physical attack. For some people, particularly those who move to a new area and are isolated from friends and family, persistent harassment can be both intimidating and psychologically damaging. They dare not step outside their homes to do the simplest things like putting out the rubbish, they dare not let their children play in the garden, their cars cannot be parked safely outside and, even in their homes, families do not feel safe. They may receive threatening phone calls, their houses can be daubed with racist messages, windows can be broken and firebombs have even been pushed through letterboxes in the dead of night.

It is estimated that half of all such attacks are carried out by school children or young people, 20% involve neighbours, half of all victims know their attackers.

Racial violence is not new; in the race riots of 1919, Charles Wootton was killed in Liverpool. And Jewish refugees to Britain put up with constant harassment at the beginning of the 20th century. Black people, particularly those who arrived in the 1950s and 1960s, when politicians were whipping up racial hatred, had to try to organise within their communities for protection against such violence. For the additional problem was that the authorities – the police, the courts and judiciary – did not understand the nature and severity of the racial violence that minorities had to

RACISM? —DON'T YOU WANT TO BE LIBERATED?!

undergo. This meant that the police did not take reports of attacks seriously, they were not properly investigated, culprits were not found. And, when they were, serious charges were not brought and magistrates and judges were often too lenient in their sentencing. The result was that minority communities lost faith in the criminal justice system and, of course, that perpetrators of violence went free.

But, since the murder of schoolboy Stephen Lawrence in 1993 and the subsequent report by Macpherson (1999) into the incompetence and racism shown by the police who were investigating this racial violence death, attempts have been made to remedy the situation. A new definition of a racial incident was suggested: 'A racist incident is any incident which is perceived to be racist by the victim or any other person.' A national Racial and Violent Crimes Task Force was set up to investigate serious racial, sexual and homophobic attacks. Racist chanting at football grounds has been made a specific offence. And in the Crime and Disorder Act, a number of new 'racially aggravated offences' were created. This stated that for certain crimes such as assault, harassment, wounding, if there was an additional racial element to the offence, the

sentences should be increased. In 2000-2001, police recorded 25,100 racially aggravated offences of which 12,455 incidents were of racially aggravated harassment, 4,711 incidents of racially aggravated common assault and 3,176 incidents of racially aggravated wounding in England and Wales.

It is estimated that half of all such attacks are carried out by school children or young people, 20% involve neighbours, half of all victims know their attackers

---

All types of racial violence in the UK remain high and the Macpherson report has had an impact – either in forcing the police to take racial violence seriously, or on prompting victims to report more cases. In the years 1994-98 reported racist incidents in the Metropolitan police area were around 5,000 year-on-year. But in the year 1998/99 the number of reported incidents rose to 11,050 (an increase of 89%) and in the year 1999/2000 the figure has more than doubled again to 23,346 (an increase of

---

In 2000-2001, police recorded 25,100 racially aggravated offences of which 12,455 incidents were of racially aggravated harassment

---

111%). In 2000/01 all racist incidents recorded by the police in England and Wales were 53,090.

Of course the number of racial attacks reported to the police may still only be a fraction of the actual attacks that take place. Another way of counting such attacks is to interview victims. According to the *British Crime Survey* there were 280,000 racially motivated incidents in 1999. 98,000 of these (i.e. 35%) were against Black, Indian, Pakistani and Bangladeshi people (who comprise 7% of the population). Those at greatest risk of racial attack are

---

The most serious of racial attacks occur when, like Stephen Lawrence, a victim is murdered

---

Pakistani and Bangladeshis at 4.2%, followed by Indians at 3.6% and Black people at 2.2%. This compared with 0.3% for white people.

The most serious of racial attacks occur when, like Stephen Lawrence, a victim is murdered.

Although such attacks are far rarer than everyday attacks of harassment, the figures are still chilling. Our research shows that in the last ten years there have been over 50 people killed in racial attacks.

Sources: Metropolitan Police Statistics; *British Crime Survey, 2000*; ESRC Violence Research Programme

■ The above information is from the Institute of Race Relations' web site which can be found at www.irr.org.uk

© *Institute of Race Relations 2002*

Victims of racial crime

Highest risk for Pakistanis/Bangladeshis

In 1999, the risk of being the victim of a racially motivated incident was considerably higher for members of minority ethnic groups than for White people.

The highest risk was for Pakistani and Bangladeshi people at 4.2 per cent, followed by 3.6 per cent for Indian people and 2.2 per cent for Black people. This compared with 0.3 per cent for White people.

Racially motivated incidents represented 12 per cent of all crime against minority ethnic people compared with 2 per cent for White people.

According to the *British Crime Survey* the estimated number of racially motivated offences in England and Wales fell from 390,000 in 1995 to 280,000 in 1999. The number of racially motivated incidents against Black, Indian, Pakistani, and Bangladeshi people also fell, from 145,000 in 1995 to

98,000 in 1999. This indicates that increased levels of racially motivated incidents, as recorded by police statistics, relate to improvements in recording and higher levels of reporting such incidents.

Emotional reactions to racially motivated incidents were generally more severe than for non-racially motivated incidents. In 1999, 42 per

cent of victims of racially motivated crime said that they had been 'very much affected' by the incident, compared with 19 per cent of victims of other sorts of crime. Black victims were most likely to report being 'very much affected', 55 per cent compared with 41 per cent for both Asian and White victims.

Indian, Bangladeshi and Pakistani

Racially motivated incidents represented 12% of all crime against minority ethnic people compared with 2% for White people

---

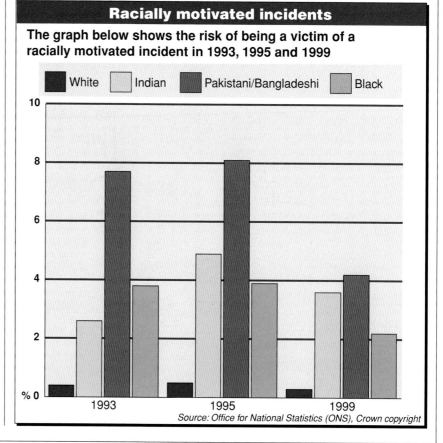

Racially motivated incidents

The graph below shows the risk of being a victim of a racially motivated incident in 1993, 1995 and 1999

White Indian Pakistani/Bangladeshi Black

Source: Office for National Statistics (ONS), Crown copyright

people are more likely to be victims of household crime than Black or White people. Indians were particularly more at risk of burglary than others.

Sources: Clancy, A., Hough, M., Aust, R. and Kershaw, C. (2001). *Crime, Policing and Justice: the experience of ethnic minorities: Findings from the 2000 British Crime Survey*, Home Office Research Study 223.

Racially motivated crime: *British Crime Survey* respondents are asked, in respect of all crimes of which they

---

'A racist incident is any incident which is perceived to be racist by the victim or any other person'

---

were victims, whether they thought the incident was racially motivated. Victims are defined as anyone who judged that racial motivation was present in any household or personal

crime which they had experienced in the relevant year, including threats. The definition is broadly in line with that recommended by the Stephen Lawrence Inquiry, which has subsequently been adopted by the police: 'A racist incident is any incident which is perceived to be racist by the victim or any other person' (Macpherson, 1999).

Household crimes include: bicycle theft; burglary; theft in a dwelling; other household theft, thefts of/from vehicles, and vandalism to household property/vehicles.

White victims of race hatred

The battle against bigotry will be lost if we ignore the white victims of race hatred

Racism and ethnic prejudice are deplorable evils and I believe that I have an absolute responsibility to condemn xenophobes and institutions which discriminate against people on grounds of their racial, religious and ethnic backgrounds.

Does that mean that I should damn black and Asian people who assault and abuse victims because they are white? Yes. Do I say this often enough? No.

This is an issue which has just been raised by Phil Woolas, a government whip whose constituency is in Oldham East. Last month, there was a noticeable increase in the number of attacks on white people in Oldham, and some undoubtedly had racist motives.

Woolas believes race relations will be damaged unless politicians, prominent people and the Commission for Racial Equality clearly condemn racist, violent attacks against white people as strongly or as forcibly as such attacks against Asian and black people.

He is now facing accusations that he is pandering to racists, even though many of his non-white constituents agree with his remarks.

By Yasmin Alibhai-Brown

Writing openly about these problems is incredibly hard if you are, as I am, an Asian (I arrived here from Uganda in the Seventies with thousands of fellow Asians fleeing the savagery of Idi Amin) and a life-long anti-racist. You know some people will brand you a traitor.

Struggle

One organisation has already withdrawn an invitation – which I had accepted – to speak at a conference on racism. Fine. But I believe that to wilfully ignore what is going on is no longer an option.

Our entire struggle against racism, its moral and ethical foundation, stands to be discredited because we are not paying enough attention to white victims of black and Asian hatred.

The most recent *British Crime Survey* figures show that there are substantial numbers of white people who feel themselves to be victims of racially motivated attacks, just as many black and Asian Britons do the other way around.

In many cases crimes may be seen as 'racial' when they are simply acts of colour-blind felony or anti-social behaviour, but that still leaves many instances where race and ethnicity are partly responsible for very real violations of black as well as white Britons.

So we need to take Mr Woolas's warning seriously – but we must exercise caution. We don't want to hand even more useful poison to neo-Fascist parties to add to their supremacist broth.

Look at the National Front web site and you'll find emotional accounts of '150 murders of innocent whites by savage, low-IQ Negroes let into the country by treacherous politicians'.

And there is always a worry that you encourage those who believe *all* victims of racism in Britain are white and that most criminals are black, or Asian.

It is, of course, unacceptable for society to revile and punish black and Asian miscreants more harshly than white scoundrels, and, appallingly, racial attacks on black and Asian people are still destroying too many lives and hopes.

Unfortunately, fighting against these injustices has created a set of new assumptions which are just as unacceptable.

Black and Asian people behaving badly are too readily excused, their crimes hidden or explained away, which is unjust, unhealthy and corrupting of the communities themselves.

Concentrating only on white racism means other forces which destroy lives are never confronted. For example, black on black violence was barely addressed until the deaths of two young black women on New Year's Day in a Birmingham shoot-out.

A *File on Four* programme on Radio 4 recently examined the flourishing heroin trade in areas of Bradford – a trade which is entirely in the hands of bandit second-generation British Muslims who, I am sure, are very devout.

We don't talk about that but real equality should mean equal rights and equal culpability.

Brutalise

We are living in the most wretched of times where bitter hatreds are stalking the streets aggressively and threatening all that is good about us as a nation.

In such times, it is hard to hold on to this, but Britain *has* come a long, long way from those days in the Fifties and Sixties when thousands of white people in London, Cardiff and Liverpool went looking for 'niggers' to brutalise and terrorise because they had dared to come and claim their place in their motherland.

White and black anti-racists have managed to keep up the battle for equality and justice through the decades.

Racism still exists and maybe always will, but we have managed to get some change within institutions (not nearly enough) – and even Tories are now enthusiastic champions of diversity.

Most encouraging of all are those intimacies – marriages, relationships and friendships – between blacks, whites and Asians, which you do not see in most other Western countries.

Black and Asian bigots do not want an integrated new Britain, and have come to believe that all whites are now fair game because of slavery, colonialism and the racism we have all experienced.

Demean

Abu Hamza, the cult leader in Finsbury Park mosque, says that he is who he is because of all the racism he faced all those years ago. Is that any reason to tolerate what he is now doing, inciting impressionable young Muslim men to oppose and demean white British cultures and faiths?

Again, we get very indignant if we discover Islamophobia – but how many Muslims rage against the anti-Christian views of so many mullahs?

If gangs of young white men openly said that black and Asian girls are easy sluts to be knocked about and used, what would anti-racists do?

Again and again I come across black and Asian men who freely express such objectionable views about young, white women who don't realise just how they are 'dissed' (disrespected) by the men they fancy, trust and even love.

As for the beatings and killings of Asian women who make the mistake of falling in love with white or black men, is that culture – or pure, murderous racism?

White supporters turn up to mourn the racist killings of black and Asian victims. So shouldn't black activists march and remember victims such as Ross Parker, a white teenager murdered in Peterborough 18 months ago by three Muslim men with a hammer and foot-long knife?

Our values are worthless unless all victims of these senseless deaths matter equally.

I am told: 'Ah, we know it is going on, but don't speak out.' But we must, because these dirty secrets do not help the cause of racial justice. In fact, they are a betrayal of that ideal.

To make a good society, all of us – black and white Britons – need to be more honest about what is happening around us, and that is the hardest thing of all.

■ A version of this article first appeared in the *Independent*.

The criminal justice system

People from ethnic minority backgrounds are effectively discriminated against three times over when it comes to crime and the whole criminal justice system

They are more likely than white people to be victims of crime; they are likely to receive much harsher penalties than their white counterparts; in terms of employment the legal establishment is almost uniformly white and ethnic minorities are under-represented in both the prison and police services.

Victims of crime

Whereas 25% of the white and black populations are likely to be victims of crime generally, Indians, Pakistanis and Bangladeshi people are more likely (at 27 and 29%) to be victims of crime. While 0.3% of white people are likely to be victims of racially motivated offences, 2.2% of black people, 3.7% of Indians and 4.3% of Pakistani/Bangladeshis are likely to be. In other words, a Bangladeshi is fourteen times more likely than a white person to be a victim of a racially motivated offence.

Creating criminals

Right through the system, from a stop on the street to the type of sentence and prison allocation, ethnic minority people are affected by racial bias. In 2001/02 of 714,000 stops and searches recorded by the police, 12% were of black people (1.8% of the population), 6% Asian (2.7% of the population). Black people were eight times more likely to be stopped and searched than white people. Compared with the previous year, searches rose 8% for whites, but 30% for black people and 40% for Asians in London. In the rest of England and Wales there was a rise of 6% for black people and 16% rise for Asians.

Figures on the ethnicity of those arrested also show ethnic minorities coming off worst. Arrests of black and Asian people rose in 2000/01 by 5 and 8% while those of white people fell by 2%. Black people were four times more likely to be arrested than white people.

And in those being let off with a caution, while 16% of white people and 17% of Asians were cautioned, only 13% of black people were. When it came to getting bail as opposed to being remanded in custody pending trial, bail was more likely for white offenders (84%) than black (71%).

That so many more black young offenders (than white) plead not guilty in magistrates and crown courts, 33 and 48% respectively (compared to 21 and 30% for whites) suggests that there may well have been a bias earlier on in the system. Certainly acquittal rates go on to suggest this. 58% of Asian young people in magistrates' courts are acquitted, 59% of blacks and only 41% of whites. This differential is repeated, if less starkly, in crown court acquittals.

Partly as a result of a whole discriminatory system, ethnic minority groups represent a disproportionate percentage of the prison population. In June 2000, ethnic minorities accounted for 19% of the male prison population (12% black, 3% Asian) and 25% of the female prison population (19% black and 1% Asian). According to an academic survey published in December 2002, black people are six times more likely to be sent to prison than whites and more likely to be imprisoned for a first offence. Almost a quarter of the 72,416 jail population came from an ethnic minority background with black prisoners accounting for 15% of all prisoners.

Employment

Relative to the population, people from minority ethnic backgrounds are under-represented in all grades as employees in the police and prison services and in all senior posts in all criminal justice agencies.

In 2001 not one Law Lord and not one High Court Judge was from an ethnic minority. Just six of the 610 circuit judges (1%) are from an ethnic minority. Just 4.8% of 33,000 magistrates are from ethnic minorities and of the 1074 Queen's Counsels (QCs – senior barristers), only 7 are black and 7 Asian. That is despite the fact that 9% of the 13,000 barristers from which QCs are drawn, are from ethnic minority groups.

Given all these facts about discrimination in the system, is it any wonder that of all complaints made against the police in 2000/01, 8% were from black people, 5% from Asians and 2% from other ethnic minority groups?

Sources: Lord Chancellor's Department, *Race and the Criminal Justice System* (Home Office, 2002); *British Crime Survey 2000, Statistics on race and the Criminal Justice System*; HM Inspectorate of Probation: Thematic Inspection Report, *Ethnic Differences in decisions on young offenders dealt with by the CPOS*; Section 95 findings No 1 (2000); Prison Statistics, England and Wales, 2000; *Observer*, 28 December 2002.

■ The above information is from the Institute of Race Relations' web site which can be found at www.irr.org.uk

© *Institute of Race Relations 2002*

Compared with the previous year, searches rose 8% for whites, but 30% for black people and 40% for Asians in London

---

Inequality in justice

Black people six times more likely to be jailed than whites. Alarming report prompts call for independent inquiry into inequitable system of justice

Black people are six times more likely to be sent to prison than whites, a new survey reveals.

It throws fresh light on the huge disparities in justice experienced by minority ethnic groups in Britain and has prompted a call for an independent inquiry.

The wide-ranging study also found that – contrary to the popular belief of ethnic communities living in a disadvantaged 'ghetto' culture – white prisoners more often came from a background that was impoverished or abusive than their black counterparts.

Black prisoners were half as likely as whites to have been taken into local authority care during childhood, to have reported violence in their homes or suffered sexual abuse.

Professor Jeremy Coid of the Royal London School of Medicine, who led the study, said the findings questioned whether black people are dealt with more harshly within the criminal justice system.

By Shahid Osmanand and Paul Harris

'It suggests they may be more likely to receive imprisonment, even though it is their first offence.'

Almost a quarter of Britain's jail population of 72,416 people come from an ethnic minority background

The study examined data on more than 3,000 prisoners and uncovered huge differences in treatment based on ethnicity. It will be embarrassing for the Government, which has to deal with an admission of institutional racism by the Crown Prosecution Service and is facing an investigation by the Commission for

Racial Equality into allegations of racism in prisons as well.

Juliet Lyon, director of the Prison Reform Trust, said the research showed a need to address racism throughout the justice system. 'It is impossible to feel confident in a criminal justice system which sanctions the disproportionate imprisonment of black people,' she said.

'There should be an independent review of the disproportionate imprisonment of people from minority ethnic groups, not because our jails are bursting at the seams, but in the interests of equality and justice.'

Almost a quarter of Britain's jail population of 72,416 people come from an ethnic minority background. Black prisoners account for 15 per cent of all prisoners and if 'black Britain' were to be a separate country it would have the highest imprisonment rate in the world.

Black people are five times more likely than white people to be stopped and searched by police and, once arrested, are more likely to be remanded in custody than other offenders charged with similar offences.

A spokeswoman for the Home Office said it was aware that black people are disproportionately represented in the criminal justice system. 'The reasons for this may be complex and are still being investigated,' she said.

■ This article first appeared in *The Observer*, 29 December 2002.

Arrests

Total arrest figures indicate that blacks are more likely to be arrested.

Arrests per 1,000 population

The *British Crime Survey* found that an estimated 1.3 million arrests for notifiable offences took place, of which 7% were of black people, 4% Asian and 1% 'other' ethnic origin. Arrests for black people, Asians and 'other' ethnic groups rose by 5, 8 and 10% respectively last year, while the number of white people arrested fell by 2%. Black people were four times more likely to be arrested than white or other ethnic groups. White people showed a higher likelihood of being arrested for burglary and criminal damage, black people for robbery and both black people and Asians for fraud, forgery and drugs.

Source: Statistics on race and the criminal justice system, © Crown copyright

We have police in our sights, says race watchdog

By Vikram Dodd

Trevor Phillips, the new head of Britain's race watchdog, yesterday said he would tackle the police over the disproportionately high number of black people they stop and search.

Mr Phillips, who takes over as chairman of the commission for racial equality this weekend, told the *Guardian* that police racial 'bias' would be 'very much in our sights'.

Official figures show black Britons are up to eight times more likely than whites to be stopped and searched.

More stops were carried out last year than before the Macpherson report was published in 1999, with ethnic minorities bearing the brunt of the increase.

In his first interview since being appointed to the post, Mr Phillips said: 'Of course it is an issue for me, we've got to get rid of the bias.

'The tens of thousands of excess stops and searches should not happen if white and black people were being stopped and searched with the same frequency.'

Mr Phillips said he could use new powers in the Race Relations Amendment Act which places a duty on public bodies to stamp out discrimination. 'The outcome of what the police do is very much in our sights,' he said.

The selection by David Blunkett of the Labour-supporting Mr Phillips led to a cronyism row. Last week Doreen Lawrence, whose son Stephen was murdered in a racist attack, said the government had lost interest in tackling racism since Mr Blunkett became home secretary, saying it was no longer on the agenda of ministers.

Mr Phillips disagreed: 'There isn't the tiniest hope in hell I would have taken this job if I thought it had fallen off the public agenda.'

He said he did not need a sympathetic home secretary to do his job. 'The home secretary doesn't give us permission to do things, my permission is the law. I don't need David Blunkett to say "oh yes you can" or "no you can't"'.

'You can't have the CRE's policy or people's access to racial equality governed by whether you fancy the home secretary or not.'

Mr Phillips said he wanted to modernise the CRE and make white people feel that tackling discrimination was in their interests.

Black and underpaid

How black workers lose out on pay

Introduction

Any examination of racial disadvantage must recognise that racial discrimination may take several forms. This disadvantage ranges from disproportionate levels of unemployment (as compared to white workers), lack of promotion opportunities and racial harassment in the workplace. These issues have been well documented over the years[1] and will also be addressed again in a joint initiative between the TUC and the CBI which will report in the late spring of 2002. This report, however, will concentrate on wage inequality in relation to race.

The report identifies three general points. Firstly, that despite nearly a generation of race relations legislation in Britain black workers continue to face inequality in pay. Secondly, whilst emphasising the commonality of discrimination based on colour, the report shows the diversity of experience within the black community. Thirdly, the report shows that whilst all sections of the black community continue to face racism some groups manage to do better than others.

Black workers' pay: The current position

This section presents data on the current pay position of black workers in relation to white workers. The section also compares pay within the black community.

Overall black workers earn less than white workers

Table 1 reveals that the overall difference between the average weekly earnings of white and black men is £97. Only Indian men come anywhere near the average weekly earnings of white men with a negative differential of £5. The largest gap is between the earnings of Pakistani and Bangladeshi men and white men which is £150 per week.

The difference in the average weekly earnings of male black workers in comparison to male white workers is not replicated when one considers the position in relation to women. Table 2 below shows how black and white women compare in average weekly earnings.

Table 2 shows that the average weekly earnings of black women are higher than that of white women with a net difference of £7 per week. This table also suggests that all black women groups, with the exception of Pakistani/Bangladeshi women, earn more on average than their white counterparts. This table also suggests that amongst black women it is the Caribbean group that is doing better than any other ethnic group with the Pakistani/Bangladeshi group faring the worst.

> ## Only Indian men come anywhere near the average weekly earnings of white men with a negative differential of £5

The overall average figure for black women shown in Table 2 is misleading. For instance, the difference between black and white women's weekly earnings is accounted for by the proportionately greater concentration of some black women in full-time jobs compared with white women. As the table shows, Pakistani/Bangladeshi women, like their male counterparts, are bottom of the league. Pakistani and Bangladeshi families significantly trail all groups in overall income levels.[4] Further anecdotal evidence would suggest that the number of black women who are involved in the low-paid informal economy is very high. This particularly relates to 'unofficial' jobs such as in cleaning and sweatshops in the garment trade.

The introduction of the NMW in 1999 has been particularly important for black workers. The Third Report of the Low Pay Commission[5] indicated that black employees were over-represented in low-paid jobs. Indeed that report also supported the finding reported above on how Pakistani/Bangladeshi employees are over-represented amongst the low paid.

In general there seems to be a mixed experience facing the black community in relation to pay. It is possible, however, to draw the following conclusions:

- Overall black workers earn less than white workers.

- Pakistani and Bangladeshi workers find themselves at the bottom of the pay league.

Summary

The report has shown that black workers continue to receive lower pay than white workers. The TUC believes that it is in the best interests of employers and trade unions as well as the economy as a whole to remove this inequity which blights the lives of many black families throughout the country.

References

1 For example the TUC Report *Black Workers Deserve Better*, 2001.
2 Heath, A and Yu, S 2001. *Explaining Ethnic Disadvantage*. Mimeo.
3 Heath. A and Yu. S. Ibid.
4 See *Households Below Average Income Survey 1999-2000*, DSS, 2001.
5 Low Pay Commission, *The National Minimum Wage. Making a Difference: The Next Steps*, Third Report of the Low Pay Commission, Vol. 2, June 2001.

- The above information is an extract from the report *Black and Underpaid* by the TUC. For more information visit their web site which can be found at www.tuc.org.uk

© *Trades Union Congress*

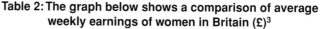

Weekly earnings

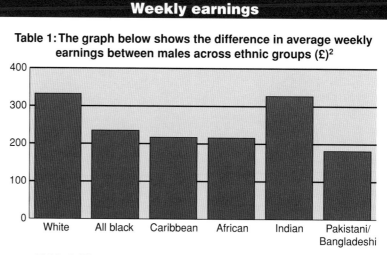

Table 1: The graph below shows the difference in average weekly earnings between males across ethnic groups (£)[2]

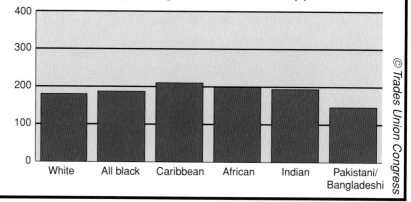

Table 2: The graph below shows a comparison of average weekly earnings of women in Britain (£)[3]

© *Trades Union Congress*

Religious discrimination and harassment

Information from Britkid

The law about this is a bit complicated, but basically there is no law protecting people from being treated badly because of their religion. The complicated bit is that, in practice, some people are protected:

- Jews are classified as a 'racial group' under the Race Relations Act because they have what's called a 'common heritage'. This means that almost all Jews are the children of Jews (it is possible to convert, but it is rare) and that people born as Jews tend to still call themselves Jews, even if they are not at all religious. Jews have also experienced such persecution that it would have been impossible not to have included them in the law. The persecution, especially under the Nazis, was not because of their religious beliefs.
- Sikhs are also classified as a 'racial group' under the Race Relations Act because they have common roots: a language and culture as well as religion in the Punjab area of north-west India. They are not physically any different from Muslims and Hindus from the same area.
- In Northern Ireland everyone is protected against discrimination at work on the grounds of their religion. Because of the history of conflict between two branches of

Mosques have been attacked, people get threats over the phone, abuse gets shouted at children, not because they are Asian but because they are Muslims

Christianity – Protestants and Catholics – the Fair Employment Act was passed. This protects people whatever their religion, so Muslims are covered too.

- Christians are protected against their religion being publicly insulted by the blasphemy laws. These were passed many years ago when almost the whole population would have said they were Christian, and when the Christian religion was much more a part of everyday life. No one has been punished for this crime for a long time, but it seems odd that it's a crime to insult the god that Christians believe in but not a crime to insult the god that Sikhs believe in.
- If some rule unfairly discriminates against a particular religion, then it may be that its followers are protected by the Race Relations Act if they all belong to one ethnic group. This is called indirect discrimination. (Example: strictly speaking it would be legal for a shop in Leicester to advertise for staff saying 'only Christians need apply', but since there are many Asian Hindus in Leicester, and not so many

Christians, they could say that indirectly the advert discriminates against them.)

Muslims are the largest religious group in Britain not protected by the law. They cannot be classed as a racial or ethnic group because Muslims do not have a long, shared history; they do not have a particular place they all come from, and they do not share a common language or a common culture. Many feel quite strongly that the law ought to protect them as Muslims, not solely as people who happen to have dark skin. Mosques have been attacked, people get threats over the phone, abuse gets shouted at children, not because they are Asian but because they are Muslims.

This may be changed because of the Human Rights Act. It may be that before long every European country has to have a law protecting people against discrimination on the grounds of their religion. This has to happen before 2006, and in Britain it may happen by the end of 2003.

- The above information is from Britkid's web site which can be found at www.britkid.org

© Britkid

Muslims in Britain

Information from Minority Rights Group International

Key issues

Since 1945, growing numbers of Muslims in Britain have moved from perceiving themselves as temporary migrants to permanent settlers. This produced challenges, not least that few models exist in Muslim history to provide guidelines for living permanently in a society with a large non-Muslim majority, and in which non-Muslim law, government and institutions predominate. British Muslims have sought to adjust to and accommodate existing institutions and practices, experimenting and negotiating between the actual and perceived demands and values of British society, and the needs, beliefs and practices of Muslims. The fact that, in some respects, their identities and values have been in conflict, or have been perceived to be in conflict, with the established norms of the non-Muslim majority population, has made the task facing Muslim communities in Britain a difficult one.

Prospects for Muslims in Britain have been circumscribed because of their low social status, lack of skills and poor education. They have been accused of ruining 'lovely' neighbourhoods, and widely blamed for causing filth and overcrowding in the poorer areas of industrial towns and cities. They have also been regarded as politically suspect, and were denounced as a 'Fifth Column' during the Gulf War, when around 200 Arabs were interned, and as

In many ways, British Muslims – British citizens, refugees or asylum-seekers – are seen as 'outsiders', marginal in their relationships to wider society and as second-class citizens

By Humayun Ansari

'terrorists' after 11 September 2001. This popular perception has periodically brought their citizenship status into question.

In contrast to Muslims resident in many Western European countries, the vast majority of British Muslims are citizens, equal before the law, and with an equal voice and vote in the political arena, but even so, many of their rights and liberties, because these are selectively administered by the state, have been attenuated. Some more recent refugees and asylum-seekers do not have citizenship or voting rights. In many ways, British Muslims – British citizens, refugees or asylum-seekers – are seen as 'outsiders', marginal in their relationships to wider society and as second-class citizens. Perhaps unsurprisingly, then, a recent poll indicated that 69 per cent of Muslims felt that 'the rest of society does not regard them as an integral part of life in Britain'.

Ethnic/religious discrimination

In the early decades of post-war Muslim settlement in Britain, discrimination tended to take an ethnic and racial form. Along with other ethnic minority groups, Muslims, especially those of South Asian origin, experienced discrimination in housing, education, employment, social and welfare services, the media and public life. There is now evidence that Muslims have also been subject to more specifically religious discrimination, which has taken a variety of forms. The nature, level of seriousness and frequency of this discrimination was identified by the Home Office report, *Religious Discrimination in England and Wales* (2001), which highlighted education, employment and the media as being the areas in which it was most

likely to occur. Some important issues were the availability of *halal* food; time off for religious festivals; refusal to allow time off for prayers; lack of or inadequate prayer facilities; and issues of dress and language in a range of settings, including schools, colleges, prisons, private and public institutions, and organisations. The report highlighted the unfair treatment of Muslims in housing, and noted occasions when planning permission was refused for mosques, schools and burial sites.

In employment, discrimination was identified over dress codes, lack of respect for and ignorance of religious customs, and in recruitment and selection practices. The wearing of the *hijab* proved problematic in schools and some workplaces. Two young Muslim women, one a solicitor and the other working in an estate agent's, recently lost their jobs because they were wearing the *hijab*. A white Muslim woman described how her work colleagues' 'mouths dropped' as she entered her office with the scarf on. Other white Muslim women were perceived as, 'comical', 'peculiar', 'very un-British', and 'a traitor to their race'. Beards too have sometimes caused problems, with examples of Muslim boys not being allowed to go to school unless they shave. Taking time off (even out of earned holiday entitlement) for Muslim religious festivals seemed, at times, to be resented by employers. And, while *halal* food has become more widely available, the response to this Muslim need by institutions is still by no means consistent. More broadly, hostility to Muslims has taken a variety of forms from abuse and discriminatory treatment to physical violence, including assaults on individuals, the desecration of graves, and attacks on mosques and other Muslim community buildings and centres.

Cultural barriers in health and social services can also disadvantage ethnic minority groups, including

Muslims. Instances of discrimination raise concerns that neither health nor social services departments adequately meet the needs of Muslims in Britain. Asylum-seekers are particularly vulnerable, as their situation is not always fully understood by the authorities, and they are often on the receiving end of negative stereotyping and assumptions.

Considerable evidence accumulated during the 1990s to reveal patterns of exclusion of Muslims from public life. A reception for aid workers, organised by Buckingham Palace and attended by 450 people, did not include any representatives of Muslim charities. Efforts have been made to change this state of affairs. The political establishment has acknowledged the Muslim presence with *Eid* parties given for British Muslims at the House of Commons and in Downing Street, but, for much of the 1990s, Muslim influence at national governmental level and in high-profile public institutions, reinforced by a perceived lack of consultation, remained minimal. On the individual level, too, Muslims are easily excluded. For example, PC Akhtar Aziz stressed in a CRE report the problems Muslims face in the police force. His colleagues 'could not understand' why he was not prepared to purchase alcohol; he 'had been treated differently' and had not been accepted.

Still, during the 1990s, despite considerable resistance, a small minority of Muslims in Britain made encouraging, albeit slow and patchy, progress in different walks of life. This was due in part to increasing acceptance of their concerns and in recognition of their contribution to British society. Some Muslims were awarded honours. A widening range of institutions recognised the benefits of overcoming the discrimination and exclusion facing Muslims, both in service delivery and in organisational life. Nevertheless, the overall situation of British Muslims remained bleak: widespread Islamophobia, manifested in prejudicial views, discriminatory policies and practices, social exclusion and different forms of violence continued. Many British Muslims feel a mixture of resentment, anger and despair, and it is not surprising that a substantial number of them remain alienated from mainstream British society. Many of the circumstances that caused disaffection in the 1960s remain essentially unaltered.

■ The above information is an extract from *Muslims in Britain*, a report by Minority Rights Group International. See page 41 for their address details.

© *Minority Rights Group International*

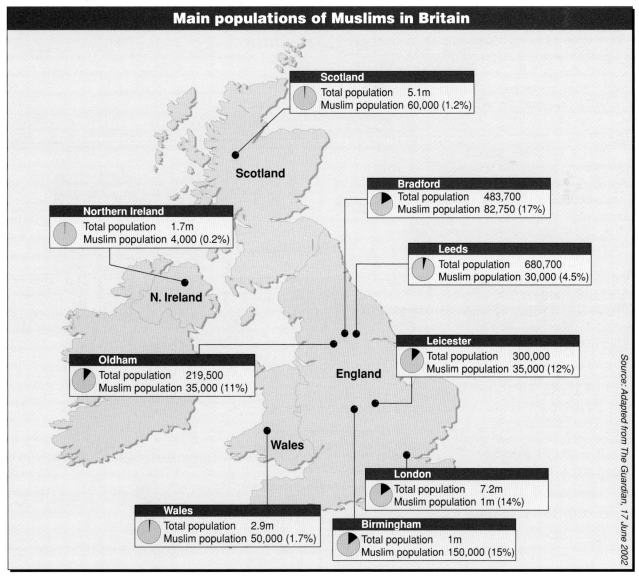

Main populations of Muslims in Britain

Scotland
Total population 5.1m
Muslim population 60,000 (1.2%)

Bradford
Total population 483,700
Muslim population 82,750 (17%)

Northern Ireland
Total population 1.7m
Muslim population 4,000 (0.2%)

Leeds
Total population 680,700
Muslim population 30,000 (4.5%)

Leicester
Total population 300,000
Muslim population 35,000 (12%)

Oldham
Total population 219,500
Muslim population 35,000 (11%)

London
Total population 7.2m
Muslim population 1m (14%)

Wales
Total population 2.9m
Muslim population 50,000 (1.7%)

Birmingham
Total population 1m
Muslim population 150,000 (15%)

Source: Adapted from The Guardian, 17 June 2002

Islamophobia

Information from Britkid

This is quite a new word in the English language and means fear of or dislike of Muslims and of their religion – Islam. It is a kind of *prejudice*. It can also become a kind of *discrimination* if people act on their prejudice, and actually treat Muslims worse as well as think about them in a worse way.

Most Muslims in Britain have roots in Pakistan, Bangladesh, India, and some African countries, with smaller numbers who have connections to Middle Eastern countries and Malaysia. This means they are very likely to be dark skinned, so ideas and actions against them can be mixed up and blurred with racism. People who are hostile towards Muslims may not be sure whether it is their religion, their colour or other things (like language) that they really dislike. Muslims who are treated badly cannot always be sure either.

At the moment discriminating against someone because they are a Muslim is not against the law.

People who dislike Muslims and Islam tend to give several reasons for this. One reason is the idea that Islam is very strict and old-fashioned, so Muslims have very hard, unbending ideas. The word usually used for this is *fundamentalist*. Actually, believers in any religion can be fundamentalist. It really means keeping very strictly to what their holy book says and not changing any rules to fit in with modern ways. Catholic Christians who say contraception is wrong could be called fundamentalists. Some Christians of various kinds believe that women cannot be priests, or that the world was created in seven days. They believe this because the Bible says so – these too could be called fundamentalists. It is not necessarily an insult, though it often seems that way.

Another reason for Islamophobia is the idea that many Muslims are terrorists. Of course this idea has grown since the attacks in the USA on 11 September 2001. These were carried out by Muslims claiming to be striking a blow against a wicked country for the sake of all Muslims. The trouble is, not all Muslims agreed with them, and many Muslim countries have joined in to try to find and punish the organisation behind the attacks.

This idea is linked to the belief that Islam allows Muslims to carry out terrorism or to kill people if they believe they are fighting a 'holy war' (Jihad in Arabic). Islam does not allow believers to do this. Many people fighting wars, whatever their religion, say they have God on their side.

Some people seem to fear that Britain is being taken over by Muslims. The page showing numbers of minority people in Britain show that British people with roots and backgrounds in Islamic countries are a long way from taking over the country. In the last election there were 15 MPs who had 10% or more of their local population who were Muslims (there are over 600 MPs altogether).

Quite a lot of ideas about Muslims and Islam come from the newspapers and TV, who tend to put over quite a limited view. The table below shows this, with a different view in each case.

■ The above information is from Britkid's web site which can be found at www.britkid.org

© Britkid

> *People who are hostile towards Muslims may not be sure whether it is their religion, their colour or other things that they really dislike*

Closed, prejudiced view of Islam	Open, unprejudiced view of Islam
Islam is seen as . . . ? the same everywhere, unchanging, unbending	*Islam is seen as . . . ?* varying in different places, with Muslims debating changes and different views
having no ideas and values in common with other faiths, and no links with them	having some shared ideas and aims and valuing communication
inferior to Europe and the USA, barbaric, primitive, sexist	different but not inferior, and worthy of respect
violent, aggressive, threatening	peaceful and maybe a partner in co-operating and solving shared problems
not European	having a long history within Europe with an influence in science and architecture
not belonging in Britain	the faith of many British, French and German people, so is here to stay
always unfairly critical of 'the West'	perhaps having a view on life and the world worth listening to
too strict, especially on girls and young people	having strong moral standards

Islamabad thing

Is religion really to blame for the disaster that threatens to turn the world upside down? Sajeel Awan investigates

The recent terrorist attack on America was a disaster of epic proportions. I don't want to take the emphasis away from the suffering because that's the most important aspect. The huge loss of human life was terrible and heartbreaking. But you all know this. You've all seen the news reports. What we need to examine now is the public response and how it will affect the peaceful co-existence that this society of ours is supposed to be so proud of.

Most people's immediate reaction was a mixture of shock, outrage and sympathy. All the natural, human emotions you'd expect. But what disturbed me, after the bewildering event had begun to sink in, was the subsequent vilification of normal, innocent Muslims.

I understand how quickly shock and pain can turn to anger and aggression. That's natural. But we must hope that people put things into perspective.

We've heard reports of Muslim cab drivers being beaten up and mosques being attacked. Some Muslims have been taunted and verbally abused while others have received hate mail and death threats. Women have been abused on the street for wearing headscarves.

Perhaps this behaviour is only a temporary, knee-jerk reaction which will subside once we've had time to come to terms with what's happened but there's a real danger of this unacceptable behaviour continuing. If so, it will only increase mistrust, tension and unrest. The riots that took place in the north of England earlier

---

Some Muslims have been taunted and verbally abused while others have received hate mail and death threats

---

in the year are just one example of the problems that might arise.

What happened in New York and Washington was a result of anger, hatred, racism and other misguided attitudes. Taking out more anger on innocent Muslims will do no one any good. If anything, it's an arrogant dishonour to the very loss of human life that we are mourning.

To hold all Muslims or people of Middle-Eastern origin responsible for the actions of a misguided minority is not only ridiculous, it is bordering on fascism.

It is the equivalent of holding all Christians accountable for the actions of General Pinochet based on the fact that he held some Christian beliefs.

I will be the first to admit that there are some arrogant, even racist Muslims but there are also arrogant Christians, Jews, Hindus and Atheists. The television coverage of Palestinians celebrating in the streets was disturbing. But it should have been made clearer that the majority of Palestinians in that region had not reacted in such a distasteful manner. In fact, the majority of Muslims, here, in the Middle East and elsewhere were as appalled as anyone else by what happened.

Islam is not united in all its beliefs. There are debates about many aspects of the religion, particularly the meaning of 'Jihad'. Depending on who you listen to, Jihad is either an obligation placed on Muslims to fight on behalf of fellow Muslims who are oppressed or mistreated, or an ongoing struggle to impose Islamic law over the world. These are obviously very different interpretations. Also, the description of Jihad as 'holy war' is not entirely accurate. Jihad is not limited to 'war' in the physical sense. It refers to an Islamic struggle that can manifest itself in forms such as teaching, writing and art. Terrorism is the extreme, not the rule.

The Taliban regime that is said to have been harbouring and supporting the terrorists of Osama Bin Laden's al-Qaeda movement is also, despite its beliefs to the contrary, in contradiction to orthodox Islam. Islam is supposed to be tolerant of all other religions. Women are supposed to have rights. The Taliban must have rewritten the Qur'an. Or read it upside down. Either way they've got it wrong.

Blind anger directed towards all Muslims or people of Arab descent will only spawn further hatred

---

Neither terrorism nor the policies of the Taliban regime are in tune with orthodox Islam. The murder of unarmed civilians, women and children is not condoned in the Qur'an or in any of the teachings of the prophet Muhammad.

Combat is supposed to be limited to face-to-face fighting against soldiers. Doesn't this make the attack on the World Trade Centre a violation of Islamic teaching?

Whoever was responsible for the attack on America, and for any acts that claim the lives of innocent people, should be made to account for their actions. Anyone who celebrates the death or suffering of another human being should be chastised for doing so. But blind anger directed towards all Muslims or people of Arab descent will only spawn further hatred and intensify the cycle that led to these horrific events in the first place.

■ The above information is from *Exposure Magazine*. Visit their web site at www.exposure.org.uk

© *Exposure*

Moving towards a just, multicultural Britain

Information from the Jewish Council for Racial Equality

Background

Multiculturalism has been defined as a situation where there are many different cultures in a society, and where the available services and facilities (for example, health education, the arts etc.) recognise this fact in a positive way.

The term describes both an approach (e.g. multicultural education) and a vision (e.g. multicultural society).

Although the term multiculturalism is used widely, it is not easy to define. Those of us who live in big cities and towns are well aware of the diversity within Britain making it a melting pot of skin colours, languages, religions, customs, and dress. For some, these differences are an accepted part of life. Others may go about their daily lives as if living in a parallel world inhabited only by their own particular group. Also, it is easy to forget that there are parts of Britain where diversity does not exist. Is it possible to share a common identity of Britishness which is at ease with diversity, regardless of where we live?

By Dr Edie Friedman

The issue of multiculturalism raises many questions, such as:

- How do we encourage children and their families to appreciate how enriching it is to live in a multicultural society without feeling threatened by it?
- How do we get across the notion that multiculturalism is not about making everyone the same, but about strengthening and appreciating one's own identity within a diverse society?
- How can we understand about differences so that we see that

These contradictions are part of the challenge we face in understanding and contributing to our multiracial society

there are as many differences within communities as there are between communities?

Part of the challenge we also face is in defining other terms such as 'ethnic minority'.

Such terms may reinforce the view that only black people have 'ethnicity', and that all white people share the same homogeneous characteristics. 'British' may be seen as synonymous with 'English', thereby ignoring the experience of Scottish, Welsh and Irish people.

Inevitably, our multiracial society is full of contradictions. The writer and broadcaster Yasmin Alibhai-Brown reminds us that Indian food now has a turnover that is higher than coal, steel and shipbuilding combined. 'The nation's favourite newsreader is Trevor MacDonald but in recent times there have been up to 250,000 racially motivated incidents every year in this country on black people, many of whom look just like him.'

These contradictions are part of the challenge we face in understanding and contributing to our multiracial society.

Things to think about

Should we describe people as
- 'British black',
- 'British Asian',
- British Jewish'?

What does 'Britishness' mean to you?

■ The above information is an extract from *Making a Difference – Promoting Race Equality in Secondary Schools, Youth Groups and Adult Education – A Jewish Perspective*, by Dr Edie Friedman, produced by the Jewish Council for Racial Equality. See page 41 for their address details.

© *Jewish Council for Racial Equality*

Your rights

Information from the Commission for Racial Equality

What is racial discrimination?

The Race Relations Act is concerned with people's actions and the effects of their actions, not their opinions or beliefs. Racial discrimination is not the same as racial prejudice. It is not necessary to prove that the other person intended to discriminate against you: you only have to show that you received less favourable treatment as a result of what they did.

To bring a case under the Race Relations Act, you have to show you have been discriminated against in one or more ways that are unlawful under the amended Act.

Direct racial discrimination

This occurs when you are able to show that you have been treated less favourably on racial grounds than others in similar circumstances. To prove this, it will help if you can give an example of someone from a different racial group who, in similar circumstances, has been treated more favourably than you. Racist abuse and harassment are forms of direct discrimination.

Indirect racial discrimination

This occurs when you or people from your racial group are less likely to be able to comply with a requirement or condition, and the requirement cannot be justified on non-racial grounds. For example, a rule that employees or pupils must not wear headgear could exclude Sikh men and boys who wear a turban, or Jewish men or boys who wear a *yarmulka*, in accordance with practice within their racial group.

Racial discrimination is not the same as racial prejudice

Victimisation

This has a special legal meaning in the Race Relations Act. It occurs if you are treated less favourably because you have complained about racial discrimination or supported someone else who has.

Am I protected in all circumstances?

No. The Race Relations Act protects you from racial discrimination in most, but not all, situations. You will therefore have to show that the discrimination you have suffered comes within the areas covered by the amended Act. On 2 April 2001, amendments to the Race Relations Act came into force which brought previously exempt public bodies within the scope of the amended Act.

The amended Race Relations Act also imposes a general duty on all public bodies to promote racial equality and eliminate racial discrimination, and gives the Home Secretary (and Scottish Ministers, in Scotland) the power to make Orders placing specific duties on some or all public bodies. The CRE will have the power to enforce these duties when they come into force towards the end of 2001, by issuing compliance notices.

Discrimination in any of the areas listed below is unlawful under the amended Race Relations Act.

Employment

The amended Act applies to most employees, including vocational trainees. You are protected if you do personal work for someone else, for example plumbing or roof repairs. Employers and employment agencies must not discriminate on racial grounds against people seeking work, and unions are under a similar duty not to discriminate against their members or those wishing to become members. Partnerships in firms with six or more partners are also covered, as are bodies responsible for conferring qualifications or authorisation to enter a particular profession.

You are protected in all aspects of employment including: recruitment, selection, promotion, transfer, training, pay and benefits, redundancy, dismissal and terms and conditions of work.

Exceptions

The amended Act does not apply to:
- certain jobs where the Crown is the employer (for example: the Bank of England, the British Museum, the British Council, embassies and consulates and certain jobs within the civil service): discrimination on the basis of nationality or ethnic or national origin is not unlawful, but discrimination based on colour is prohibited
- work that is for the purpose of a private household
- work where race is a 'genuine occupational qualification' for the job; such as acting, modelling or serving in cafés or restaurants, where people from a particular ethnic or racial background are needed for authenticity; or providing personal welfare services to people of a particular racial group which are best provided by a person from that racial group
- jobs that involve working outside Great Britain most of the time.

Education

The amended Act applies to all schools and colleges maintained by local education authorities or education authorities (in Scotland), independent (fee paying) schools and colleges, further education colleges, special schools, early years providers, universities, local education authorities and governors of schools and colleges and school boards (in Scotland). The amended Act covers admission, treatment as a pupil or student, and exclusion, as well as decisions by local education authorities and education authorities (in Scotland), such as decisions on special educational needs.

Housing

The amended Act applies to the selling, letting or managing of property (including business premises), making it illegal to discriminate in the way any of these activities are conducted.

Exceptions

The amended Act does not apply to rental accommodation in 'small premises' where the landlord/ landlady or owner, or a member of his or her family, also live, and where they would have to share facilities with people who are not members of the household

Goods and services

The amended Act applies to anyone providing goods, facilities or services to the public; for example: hotels, shops, banks, insurance companies, financial services, cinemas, theatres, bars, restaurants, pubs, places of entertainment or refreshment, transport and travel services, and services provided by any local or public authority and by any profession or trade. It is unlawful to be refused a service, or not to be given the same standard of service extended to others.

Exceptions

The amended Act does not apply to:
- taking in and caring for foster children or elderly people
- clubs, associations and charities set up especially for people from a particular ethnic or national group; discrimination on the basis of nationality or ethnic or national origin is not unlawful, but discrimination based on colour is prohibited

Any public function

From 2 April 2001, the amended Act applies to all the functions of public authorities that were previously excluded. This brings within the scope of the amended Act the law enforcement or control functions of government agencies, including the police, the Crown Prosecution Service, the probation service, Customs and Excise, the immigration service and the prison service; and the regulatory functions of local

JUST BETWEEN YOU AND ME — THE SCHOOL DOWN THE ROAD IS BETTER THAN THIS ONE...

ENROLMENTS

authorities, including environmental health, trading standards, licensing, and child protection. If you believe you have been discriminated against, directly, indirectly or by way of victimisation, by any public authority since 2 April 2001, you have the right to bring a complaint in a county court in England and Wales or in a sheriff court in Scotland. Certain complaints of discrimination relating to decisions on immigration status will be considered as part of the one-stop immigration appeal procedure.

You are also protected against discrimination where a public function is being carried out by a private company or a voluntary organisation on behalf of a public authority. This means the amended Act applies to prison discipline in private prisons as well as prisons run by the Prison Service.

Exceptions

The amended Act does not apply to:
- the work of the Houses of Parliament or the security services
- judicial or legislative acts and decisions not to prosecute
- certain immigration and nationality functions where discrimination is permitted on grounds of nationality or ethnic or national origin

---

You are also protected against discrimination where a public function is being carried out by a private company

---

Additional areas outside the scope of the amended Act

The following areas are also outside the scope of the amended Act:
- anything written, produced or broadcast by the media — the law of libel applies only to individuals, not to groups of people
- anything done under 'statutory authority' in order to comply with an Act of Parliament (whenever it was passed), or rules or regulations made by a government minister under any law; for example, a parent's choice of school may be racially discriminatory, but quite lawful under the education laws
- racist attacks or harassment on the street or in your home; these could be criminal offences and should be reported to the police
- discrimination that occurs in other countries of the EU; however, many countries have their own laws against racial discrimination. The EU race directive, approved in June 2000, will require all EU countries to introduce laws outlawing racial discrimination by July 2003
- discrimination on grounds of religion; however, you may be protected by the Race Relations Act if the discrimination is also on the ground of your national or ethnic origin

Are racial harassment, abuse and violence covered?

You are protected by the Race Relations Act if you have been abused or harassed on racial grounds in any of the situations covered by the amended Act. For example, you can bring a case against your employer if you experience racist abuse from other employees, or from customers or clients, and your employer does nothing to put a stop to it or to protect you from such abuse. You may be able to take a case against your landlord or landlady if you are racially harassed by them or by their employees.

In situations not covered by the Race Relations Act, you may be able to use other laws to get the harassment or abuse stopped. For example,

if you are racially harassed by your neighbours, their visitors or others in the local community, you or your local council may be able to get a court order to stop the harassment. If the people who are harassing you live in a rented property, the landlord or landlady may be able to take action to evict them. Of course, you should also report all incidents to the police.

Racist attacks and violence are serious criminal offences and must be reported to the police. The Crime and Disorder Act 1998 created new 'racially aggravated offences', such as harassment, assault, grievous bodily

harm, and criminal damages, which carry significantly higher penalties. It is also a criminal offence under the Public Order Act 1986 to use threatening, abusive or insulting language or behaviour in order to stir up racial hatred. This includes distributing racist leaflets. All suspected criminal offences and any racist incident should be reported to the police.

■ The above information is from the Commission for Racial Equality's web site which can be found at www.cre.gov.uk

© Commission for Racial Equality

Racial harassment

What is racial harassment and where to report incidents of harassment

What is racial harassment?

'Racial harassment' is not recognised by existing law, though 'harassment' is a criminal offence, and is punishable in certain circumstances. In addition, 'incitement to racial hatred' is an offence under the Public Order Act, though this cannot at present be prosecuted without the consent of the Attorney General. Nowhere in law are the two aspects of racial harassment clearly bought together.

The Macpherson Inquiry into the death of Stephen Lawrence recommended that the definition of a racist incident is as follows; 'A racist incident is any incident which is perceived to be racist by the victim or any other person' (p. 328).

This definition has been adopted by the Metropolitan Police and is now their criterion for determining a racist incident. This means that if you or another person tell a police officer that you perceive an incident to be racist then they must investigate and record as such. The Inquiry report also recommended that this definition should be universally adopted by local authorities and other statutory agencies.

Racial harassment can occur in a number of ways, for example:

■ Unprovoked assaults including common assault; actual bodily harm; and grievous bodily harm.
■ Damage to property including:

breaking windows, doors and fences and within the perimeter of the house.
■ The daubing of slogans and/or graffiti of a racial nature within or in the proximity of the perimeter of the house concerned.
• Arson or attempted arson.
• The insertion of rags, paper, rubbish and/or any material which can be and/or has been set alight through openings, or within the perimeter of the property concerned.
■ The insertion of excrement, eggs, paint, faeces, rubbish and/or other noxious and/or offensive substances through an opening in the house concerned or within its perimeter.
■ The sending of threatening and/or abusive telephone calls of a racial nature.
■ Verbal racial abuse.

Racial harassment can occur in a number of ways, for example, unprovoked assaults including common assault; actual bodily harm; and grievous bodily harm

---

■ Demanding money accompanied by verbal abuse.
■ Repeated vandalism of a property belonging to the person concerned or any member of his/her household.
■ Threatening and abusive behaviour including spitting.
■ Participation in any activity which is calculated to deter the person from occupying a particular property.
■ Attempted murder or murder.

Where to report incidents

You should report racial harassment as soon as you can. The Macpherson report recommended that the police and local authority should encourage the reporting of racist incidents 24 hours a day. You can report incidents to:
■ Your local police station
■ Your local authority
■ The Monitoring Group. Call us on 020 8834 2333 or Freephone 0800 374 618.

Remember you should report all racist incidents as quickly as possible

■ The above information is from the Monitoring Group's web site which can be found at www.monitoring-group.co.uk

© The Monitoring Group

You can do something

For better mutual understanding and against xenophobia, anti-Semitism and racism

Personal meetings, personal experience, better knowledge and more commitment can contribute decisively to changing attitudes and opinions. This holds particularly true for people's positions toward ethnic, religious and cultural minorities and asylum seekers.

You can help to bring about such a change, alone or together with others. There is a lot you can do – in every sphere of life.

For life with cultural, ethnic and religious diversity in Europe; because Europe's future, its opportunities and its richness depend on this diversity.

Every positive action, small as it may be, is an important contribution towards improving the situation.

We would like to make a few suggestions.

In public

- If you hear somebody making xenophobic jokes or insulting ethnic, religious and cultural minorities, try to intervene.
- Do not tolerate discriminatory and demagogic language in discussions on ethnic, religious and cultural minorities and refugees.
- Point out that nobody would leave his/her home if he/she was not forced to do so, and that the causes for fleeing from a country are manifold.
- Try to help to give ethnic, religious and cultural minorities more say in the communities they live in. Give minorities and refugees the opportunity to meet locals and to exchange information (via sports, clubs, integration into communal and municipal life).
- Write readers' letters against xenophobic actions and reports in the media. Speak up for improving the relations between ethnic minorities and natives and the way they live together.
- Call upon MPs or representatives of your constituency to take a clear stance against xenophobia,

right-wing extremism and anti-Semitism; a politician's attitude serves as a model for the general public.

- Ask party representatives if they support the 'Charter of the European Political Parties for a non-Racist Society'.
- Get in touch with the media if they use language and pictures that create or foster xenophobia or racism.
- Take seriously people around you who express their fears and problems with respect to immigrated fellow-citizens.
- Try to address their fears and problems, and put forward arguments to invalidate them. Not everyone who expresses concern is necessarily a xenophobe.
- Try to foster initiatives within your neighbourhood. Within the

---

If you hear somebody making xenophobic jokes or insulting ethnic, religious and cultural minorities, try to intervene

---

framework of such initiatives the people concerned could come together and discuss problems and fears in connection with the accommodation of, for instance, asylum seekers. Try to address possible problems together and get in touch with NGOs, campaigning organisations, churches and similar institutions to try and help you solve them.

- Lay a charge with the police if you hear people singing right-wing extremist songs or see people playing right-extremist computer-games. Write letters to your local politicians to inform them about such right-wing extremist activities.

Within your city or municipality

- Demand that more attention is given by the municipal authorities to better understanding of and communication with minorities, particularly in the field of culture. Every cultural institution should attach particular attention to the way people deal with everything 'foreign' and should foster mutual understanding between the various cultures. For instance, the culture of ethnic minorities should also find representation in theatres, museums and concerts, and more consideration should be given to immigrated performers.

- Try to persuade associations and clubs to welcome ethnic, religious and cultural minorities and refugees. Foreign nationality is often the reason for being refused membership of a club.
- Try to establish social links between representatives of business, the unions, culture, the sciences, the churches, campaigners, the state and politicians. Representatives from all spheres of life have to get together and have round-table talks or discuss in working groups how to combat xenophobia at every level of society and to promote living together peacefully.
- Organise events or participate in events which foster mutual understanding or support initiatives of ethnic minorities. Examples for such events are the 'Refugees' day', 'Human Rights' Day' or 'The United Nations' Day against Racism'.

In your neighbourhood

- Ensure, together with others or alone, that racistic, xenophobic or anti-Semitic slogans are removed from bridges, walls and other places. Converse with people and explain why you do so.
- Support initiatives in your immediate neighbourhood which aim at promoting better understanding and combating xenophobia. NGOs can also offer valuable contributions in this context.
- Try to establish and strengthen your personal ties with ethnic, religious and cultural minorities and asylum seekers. Take the opportunity of meeting people, e.g. at cultural events or in clubs, and maybe invite them to visit you.
- Support activities which serve to protect minorities and refugees from attacks.
- Support activities or action weeks in your neighbourhood and encourage cultural institu-

---

Try to celebrate as many religious feasts as possible together with members of other religions

---

tions, independent groups, municipal authorities or local catering outlets to take part. Such events may cover any sphere of life; suggest to the organisers that they invite well-known guests to participate in these events.

- Help minorities and refugees to organise their lives, and support NGOs.

In kindergartens and schools

- Ask kindergarten and school teachers what they do to foster a better mutual understanding in kindergartens and in class and how they address racism, xenophobia and anti-Semitism in their daily work. When talking to teachers or other parents at class meetings or school conferences, support the intercultural approach in teaching.
- Suggest class outings to other countries and students' sponsorships.
- Ask teachers to discuss with their students how 'cultural understanding' is dealt with in school books and ask school authorities if this subject is included in the syllabus. Share your views with e.g. educational authorities and publishers and inform them on the outcome of such an enquiry.
- Suggest putting up posters in schools or organising exhibitions.
- School classes could go to homes for refugees and asylum seekers and talk with the people on the spot. Discuss this idea with the competent authorities.
- Suggest inviting foreign authors who represent minorities to give readings at schools.

In your religious community

- Try to celebrate as many religious feasts as possible together with members of other religions.

- Talk to and have discussions with people of different religious denomination.
- Try to encourage the members of your religious community to organise events, e.g. invite members of other religious groups to talk about their religion.
- Suggest saying political prayers on Sundays and religious holidays. Take advantage of up-coming religious feasts to advocate better mutual understanding and to stand up for it in public.

In your job

- You must ensure that all workplaces have effective equal opportunities policies that can be measured.
- Tell your colleagues during lunch or coffee breaks why you advocate better mutual understanding and oppose xenophobia.
- Suggest to your municipal authorities that they call upon companies to give ethnic, religious and cultural minorities better employment opportunities. Mutual contact in companies helps to reduce prejudice.
- As company journals are an important means of communication, invite authors to contribute in their articles to better mutual understanding and to stand firm against xenophobia. The extent to which the first article of the Human Rights Convention – 'All human beings are born free and equal in dignity and rights' – is really applied could be illustrated by a number of examples in this context.

Try to get information on the situation of ethnic, religious and cultural minorities, of refugees and people who seem to be foreign. The various local initiatives, NGOs, associations but also governmental organisations will provide you with information material.

- The above information is from the European Monitoring Centre on Racism and Xenophobia's web site which can be found at eumc.eu.int

Race the future

If our parents don't teach us that racism is wrong then who will? Sonev Karayel investigates

This is a true story. Anne is a Chinese girl aged 15 who goes to a school in Haringey. She was racially abused by a group of young people from a variety of ethnic groups. She didn't fit in with any group at school and she was always bullied about her culture. People would call her names like 'slanty eyes' or 'flat face'. Anne told one of her teachers but she didn't seem to take the situation seriously. Anne was told to ignore the abuse and that it would go away. Anne tried. It didn't.

You can imagine how hard it is for someone like Anne who doesn't belong. Anne thought that if she behaved differently then maybe other people would start to accept her. So Anne changed the way she looked. She started to listen to a different kind of music and started to smoke. A few months later Anne had made some friends but some people were still racist towards her.

Anne is a girl who gave up her own personality, even started abusing her body with cigarettes just so she could fit in; just so she wouldn't be victimised.

If someone is getting racially abused, teachers usually just tell the person that's doing it to stop. They say things like 'you should know better' and 'don't your parents teach you anything?'

But what if your parents don't teach you? They might not have time to sit down and tell us what's wrong with racism. They might not think it's important or they might even be racists themselves. So, if our parents don't tell us the difference between right and wrong and our schools don't either then WHO DOES?

Perhaps our parents and teachers need to find time to take a closer look at this issue. Maths and English, History and Geography are all important subjects but how about things like morality and humanity?

Perhaps schools could invite people a few years older than us who had experienced racism or bullying, to talk to us about how these kinds of things affected them while they were growing up. We would understand better from someone who had been through this kind of abuse and could explain their feelings in a language we could understand. The same idea is already used for tackling problems such as drugs and teenage pregnancy.

Another idea is to have someone in school all the time to talk to us about things like racism, abuse, bullying, crime and other problems. Someone who is understanding, who can listen, who we can talk to. Someone we can trust and look up to. This person could give students advice and counselling. If you were a victim of abuse this person would try and get involved to solve the problem.

As young people we also have a role to play. Those of us who do understand the difference between right and wrong need to speak up. If our friends or classmates are racist to others we should tell them to stop or let a teacher know.

As young people we also have a role to play. Those of us who do understand the difference between right and wrong need to speak up

Usually racists and bullies are those who are most insecure about themselves. They pick on people who are different to make themselves feel better.

Wouldn't you feel guilty if you just walked away from someone who was being victimised and did nothing about it? If not, why not? We all have a duty to prevent abuse. If not, we're a part of the problem too.

We're all human and we all have feelings. So what if someone is black and someone else is white? So what if someone likes pop and someone else likes R&B? If we were all the same and looked the same life would be boring.

Our differences are what make us who we are as individuals and ultimately make life more interesting for everyone else.

This message needs to be drummed into young people from an early age. Then racism can be taught in the place where it belongs – history.

For information or help regarding racism contact the Commission for Racial Equality on 020 7828 7022 or www.cre.gov.uk

If you have been the victim of racial harassment in Haringey contact Haringey Racial Equality Council on 020 8889 6871.

■ The above information is from *Exposure Magazine*. Visit their web site at www.exposure.org.uk

© *Exposure*

New unit to 'root out police racism'

By Philip Johnston, Home Affairs Editor

A new anti-racism unit is to be set up at the Home Office in response to figures showing that black people are eight times more likely to be stopped and searched by police than whites.

Police will also be required to record the ethnic details of everyone they stop amid suspicions among ministers that attempts to reduce alleged discrimination in the criminal justice system have been unsuccessful.

The number of stop and searches – which fell after the Macpherson report denounced 'institutional racism' in the Metropolitan police three years ago – is on the increase.

In the 12 months to April, there were 714,000 stop and searches in England and Wales compared to 686,000 in the previous year. Black people were eight times – and Asian people three times – more likely to be stopped than a white person last year. Black people were also four times more likely to be arrested than whites or other ethnic minority groups.

In London compared with the previous year, the number of stop and searches rose by eight per cent for white people, 30 per cent for black people and 40 per cent for Asians. In the rest of England and Wales, two per cent fewer whites were stopped and searched, while there was a six per cent rise for blacks and a 16 per cent increase for Asians.

The rise in searches coincided with a rapid increase in street crime and special operations aimed at reducing muggings and robberies. Some officers blame the explosion in street crime on the earlier fall in stop and searches caused by the post-Macpherson backlash. Police, especially in London, also maintain that most of the street crime is committed by young black men.

Earlier this month, Ian Blair, deputy commissioner of the Met, said nearly two-thirds of muggings were carried out by those described by victims as Afro-Caribbean. 'We have to be honest about this,' he said.

However, John Denham, Home Office minister, said the latest figures raised a number of questions that the unit was being set up to try to answer.

'We must get to the bottom of these issues. Where we are seeing the results of continuing discrimination we must work together to root it out. It is vital that the public engage in a serious debate about race in the criminal justice system.'

The Government has also decided to press ahead with plans to require the police to ask those stopped to give their name and address and 'self-define' their ethnicity. They will then have to provide a written record giving the reason for the stop and its outcome.

This will apply to all cases in which officers ask people to account for their actions. Police currently only record stops which result in searches.

Mr Denham said the new procedure – recommended by Macpherson – would be introduced on a pilot basis next April in Merseyside, Nottingham, Sussex, West Midlands, West Yorks, North Wales and the Metropolitan Police.

However, the Police Federation, which represents 128,000 front-line officers, says the measure will increase paperwork when the Home Office is trying to cut red tape.

The latest stop-and-search figures – whose publication was delayed by eight months – reignited the row over racism in the police that exploded around the publication of the Macpherson report into the murder of Stephen Lawrence.

The latest stop-and-search figures reignited the row over racism in the police that exploded around the publication of the Macpherson report into the murder of Stephen Lawrence

Sgt Ray Powell, general secretary of the National Black Police Association, said: 'They will reaffirm people's beliefs that the police service is institutionally racist. Police officers are reverting back to their old ways.'

Beverley Bernard, acting chairman of the Commission for Racial Equality, said there was continued racial discrimination throughout the criminal justice system. 'The message of the Stephen Lawrence report three years ago is sadly as relevant now as it was then.'

Neville Lawrence, the father of the murdered teenager, said: 'We know what the problem is and we don't need another team to sort it out.'

© Telegraph Group Limited, London 2003

Questions

1. What does the word racism mean?
2. What is the policy of 'stop and search'?
3. Why do some people believe the police are racist?
4. What argument would the police put forward to challenge the accusation of racism?
5. To what extent does this report support the view of Sgt Ray Powell that the police service is 'institutionally racist'?

A *fair cop?*

From the Scarman report to the Macpherson inquiry, the problems of racism in the police have been well documented. But what is being done to challenge the views of officers? *Guardian* crime correspondent Nick Hopkins is the first journalist to take part in a course that aims to help them confront their prejudices

There we were. A group of white men wearing suits and ties, sitting in awkward silence. In front of us, in a semicircle, six black students. The teenagers seemed a bit nervous, but gradually found their voices as they explained, in a matter-of-fact way, what life was like for them. How it is, how it was, and how they expected it to be in the future is defined by a single, ugly word – racism.

Stop and search? 'Where do I start?' said Daniel. 'I get it all the time. I was thrown against the wall once, when I was 13. It's not right . . . I'd done nothing wrong and I've never had an apology.'

For Joe, everything changed at secondary school. Before that, he hadn't been aware of any prejudice. As he got older, he was embarrassed and irritated to find that he was being picked on simply, it seemed, because of the colour of his skin.

Maxine, an older woman, had had a petrol bomb put through her letter box and 'nigger' scrawled on her house. Would any of them think of joining the police? They laughed and laughed.

The joke was not lost on the men in suits who were all – apart from me – in the hierarchy of the country's biggest force. Hearing the students speak so dispassionately about their experiences, and so disparagingly about certain officers, was a slap in the face, one of several during a two-day course designed to challenge racism and other intolerance within the Metropolitan Police.

Introduced following the Macpherson inquiry into the death of Stephen Lawrence three years ago, the course, the only one of its kind in Britain, has been a source of huge resentment to some, particularly among the junior ranks. A few have assumed that being ordered to take part is tantamount to being branded a bigot.

On previous courses officers have grudgingly turned up, but their attitude has quickly betrayed the racism that the force is desperately trying to challenge.

Stop and search? 'Where do I start?' said Daniel. 'I get it all the time. I was thrown against the wall once, when I was 13'

'I've had officers not say a single word to me in two days,' said Tony Warner, an independent consultant who is one of the course teachers. 'You can feel the hostility. They are looking at you thinking: "Why is this black man lecturing me?" Some have not looked at me at all.'

His colleague, Laurie Young, a sergeant who helped devise the programme, recalls how one officer told him flatly: 'Stephen Lawrence gets on my nerves.' Another demanded that Britain's 'Sikhs should go home'.

'When I asked him about this, I realised he didn't know the difference between a Sikh and a Muslim. There is a tremendous amount of ignorance and anger out there.'

But the two teachers insist that these people and their extreme, racist views represent a very small minority. For most Met officers and civilian staff – more than 40,000 have been involved – the course is a humbling, occasionally shocking, experience. Feedback suggests it is the most valued the Met has ever undertaken.

No 'outsider' has ever been allowed to observe the training and the Met was not going to bend the rules for the *Guardian*. Instead, the force insisted that if we wanted to

The racist paranoia about the country being 'swamped' by blacks and Asians has been around for centuries

---

see how it worked, I should take part. Other members of the group were not to be identified, for fear that this would prevent them from being open and honest about their attitudes.

It began at 9am on a Monday in a conference room at the University of Westminster. Eighteen Met officers and managers had been expected, but six dropped out when they were told that the *Guardian* was coming along. Four others didn't turn up on the day.

Warner and Young asked us in turn to describe who we were and what experiences we had of different races and cultures. We all mentioned something – trips abroad and friends were the most common. But most of our answers to a cultural quiz (see below) soon after put all this combined knowledge in rather shameful perspective. None of us was absolutely sure about anything in the few minutes we were given to choose. Put on the spot, we got in a tangle over even the simplest questions.

The largest ethnic minority group in London? Well, it isn't Afro-Caribbean, or Indian or Pakistani. It's Irish. I got three of the five pillars of Islam but was guessing over the main Hindu castes, and symbols of Sikhism. We all were.

And rather than make an idiot of myself, I kept quiet when I wasn't sure. We all did.

This meant that there were awkward, near excruciating silences when Warner asked us what we thought. If the point of the exercise was to highlight our collective ignorance, it worked very nicely and left us a little subdued.

Not a bad time, then, for Warner to tell us that racist paranoia about the country being 'swamped' by blacks and Asians has been around for centuries. Queen Elizabeth I,

Test of faith

Some of the quiz questions that the police have to answer on the course . . .

1 The following beliefs of the Islamic religion are true . . .
a) Men and women are equal
b) Women have a right to independent ownership of property and income
c) Men are superior to women
d) Islam is not a religion, but a complete way of life
Answer: (all are true, except c)

2 To gesture with one's finger as a way of beckoning or asking someone to come to you may be particularly offensive to which of the following groups.
a) African/Caribbean
b) Somalian
c) Hindus
d) Sikhs
Answer: (Somalian – it is the way that they call their dogs to heel)

3 True or false?
a) The caste system has close links to a person's occupation
b) Muslims are required to eat halal meat but can also eat kosher meat in extreme circumstances . . .
c) Sikh men may carry a kirpan (dagger) in public as long as it is accompanied by the four other symbols of Sikhism
d) Muslims who have died must normally be buried within 48 hours of death?
Answer: (a) True (b) True (c) True (d) False (it's 24 hours))

apparently, said in 1596 that there were 'too many here and they should go back where they came from'. The *Daily Mail* has been running scare stories about asylum seekers since the 1900s, he says. (Obligingly, the *Mail*'s front-page headline the following day screams: 'One in every 20 people living in London is a refugee or an asylum seeker.')

Warner reminded the group that racism in the police is nothing new, either. We were shown a video of the former Labour ministers James Callaghan and Roy Jenkins describ-

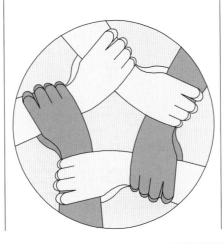

ing how the police managed to exempt themselves from the provisions of the 1976 Race Relations Act, which meant that they were not bound by law to behave in a non-discriminatory way. Jenkins recalled a meeting of the Metropolitan Police Board at which he was roundly booed and heckled for suggesting that the police should be included. Callaghan admitted that the government caved in to the bullies, and was wrong to do so.

Police are now subject to the act – but it took the Brixton riots, the Scarman report, the stabbing of Stephen Lawrence, Macpherson's inquiry and 24 years of prevarication before a Labour government was prepared to force the issue two years ago. We were left to mull over this during lunch, then Young delicately steered us towards more sensitive waters.

Assess your life and background, he asked. Take a hard look at the behaviour, attitudes, beliefs and values of your family and friends. 'My dad was a desert rat in the second world war', he said. 'I remember

---

sitting in front of the television and him laughing at Alf Garnett. That kind of stuff is going on around us all the time. It must have an effect. Do you know your prejudices? Everyone in this room has them, even if they are in our subconscious, where a lot of our memories are stored.'

I was pretty sure Young was telling us that we were all likely to be racists. This has nothing to do with working for the police and everything to do with living in a society that has consistently discriminated against ethnic minorities.

'It might just be ignorance and fear. Maybe they don't realise how much their attitude offends black people.'

The second day began tensely. A detective chief inspector, who had been with us the day before, had had to pull out because his son was ill. And at least two of the remaining members were unhappy – not about what they had heard but, if anything, that the course was not tough enough. 'It could be more stimulating,' said Phil, who has worked for the Met for more than 30 years.

Everyone thought it was pitiful that so many people – the DCI excepted – had dropped out. One of them, they had learned, had gone to the wrong place the day before and decided not to come late, an excuse they considered pathetic.

And they worried that some of the Met's most senior people pay lip service to fighting racism and that meaningful change will only come when these officers stop worrying about how they can advance their own careers.

'There is a small circle of influence,' said Steve. 'And we're not in it.'

The teenagers who came to speak to the group knew exactly how they felt, but their experiences were far more profound and suggested that the force – for all its strides in recent years – still has some way to go.

The youths, who are volunteers, are struggling to trust the police. They complained of rudeness and bad attitude and had a constant fear of being victimised. Yet they showed no anger. They didn't believe that racism was solely a problem for the police, or that all officers are racist. They didn't even want to believe that those in uniform with prejudices are incapable of change.

'It might just be ignorance and fear,' said one hopefully. 'Maybe they don't realise how much their attitude offends black people.'

Maxine took a harder line. She said that she hadn't noticed any changes on the street since the Macpherson report, and that a two-day race awareness course wasn't going to solve the problem. 'This is brushing the surface.'

The afternoon finished with a gallop through the low points of Britain's racist past, which Warner hoped would help us understand why people from ethnic minorities 'feel the way they do'. How many people were taken from west Africa to the Caribbean on slave ships? 'Between 10 and 12 million. When slavery was abolished in the mid-19th century, the plantation owners received £20m in compensation from the government for loss of their cheap labour.'

And he asked whether anyone remembered the campaign slogan of Peter Griffiths, a prospective Tory MP in the Midlands who fought – and won – a seat in Smethwick at the 1964 general election with the slogan: 'If you want a nigger for a neighbour, vote Labour.'

Mal Hussein's experiences in Lancaster, where he and his wife own a corner shop, provided the gruesome finale. In nine years, Mr Hussein was subjected to more than 500 racist incidents, including being shot at, yet the police and the council failed to protect him. In a moving video interview, Mr Hussein broke down in tears. It was a powerful end to the two days and the group broke up without much chat.

Assess your life and background. Take a hard look at the behaviour, attitudes, beliefs and values of your family and friends

---

Warner was quite pleased; he thought it had been a good course. Nobody said anything racist or balked at any of the ideas. But everybody had left saying that they had learned something. And though the teenagers couldn't see an end to the discrimination they face, they were encouraged that the Met wanted to listen.

'At least they're trying to do something about it,' said one of the boys. 'This isn't a problem for the police. It's a problem for society. But who else is making the effort?'

© *Guardian Newspapers Limited* 2003

New action by prosecutors to stamp out hate crimes

Community groups will be asked how the Crown Prosecution Service could improve the way it handles racially and religiously aggravated crime in a consultation exercise.

Attorney General, Lord Goldsmith, QC said: 'Persecuting a person for the colour of their skin, their ethnicity or their religion, is not just an attack on an individual, it is an attack on their identity, their community and their democratic freedoms.'

> **'Those who have experience of these types of crime have expertise that we need to tap'**

The CPS is asking for comments on the way it handles race and religiously aggravated crimes from the time it becomes involved, right through the criminal justice process.

Lord Goldsmith said, 'This is a nation where all communities are welcomed and valued, they add to the rich fabric of our society. A society where its citizens have no confidence in the delivery of justice, cannot be regarded as truly democratic.

'Those who have experience of these types of crime have expertise that we need to tap. The consultation is a crucial first step in developing a credible public policy statement that will meet the needs of individuals when prosecuting cases which involve either racism or religious discrimination.'

Director of Public Prosecutions, Sir David Calvert Smith, QC said: 'We need to be leaders within the criminal justice system by tackling racially and religiously aggravated crimes. It is crucial that our prosecutors have a thorough understanding of the nature of these crimes so that they are able to prosecute vigorously, give support to victims and bring the perpetrators of these crimes to book.

'We are committed to working with community groups and organisations to build trust and confidence so that victims are more likely to report crimes and help bring criminals to justice. It is our wish that through this we will reduce the justice gap between the number of recorded crimes and the number of offenders convicted.'

> **'This is a nation where all communities are welcomed and valued, they add to the rich fabric of our society'**

The consultation exercise particularly addresses the question of how additional support can be given to victims. It asks respondents to comment on issues including:

- What measures would encourage victims and witnesses to pursue the case through the criminal justice process;
- How best to keep victims and witnesses informed of the criminal process; and
- How best to communicate outcomes of cases to the wider community.

■ The above information is from the Crown Prosecution Service's web site which can be found at www.cps.gov.uk

© Crown Copyright 2003

Fly the flag against racism

Blunkett prepares battle against 'race glass ceiling' and says far right must not regain national symbol

The British, and in particular the English, need to sustain their efforts to 'reclaim the flag', begun during the golden jubilee and World Cup, to see off the British National Party and the National Front, David Blunkett said last night.

In a speech to the Social Market Foundation, in which he outlined an agenda for tackling racism, the home secretary said 'covert racism and glass ceilings' were 'often the modern face of racism'.

Mr Blunkett distanced himself from the reported comments of David Calvert-Smith, the director of public prosecutions, by saying that the 'vast majority of people in this country are not racists'. In talking about 'covert racism', he did, however, acknowledge the arguments about 'institutional racism'.

> **'It is encouraging that a recent Mori poll demonstrated that 86% of people disagreed that you have to be white to be British'**

He added that even where ethnic minorities were 'as well qualified' as members of the white community, they did not succeed to the level expected in the labour market and wider society. 'Taking age, educational qualifications and geography into account, a black male has only a third of the chance of a white male of being in a professional job. An Indian male has only three-fifths of the chance, and a Pakistani or Bangladeshi male about half the chance.'

But in confronting such 'covert racism' it was necessary not only to tackle individual prejudice head on, but also to combat the class inequalities faced by minority ethnic groups in jobs, housing, education, income and assets.

By Alan Travis, Home Affairs Editor

Amid an increasingly emotional debate over asylum and refugees, Mr Blunkett also stressed the positive benefit of 'economic migrants' to Britain and called for a consensus to support new legal routes of entry for those wanting to work in the UK.

The widespread use of the flag of St George and the union flag across England in recent weeks, particularly to back a multicultural England team in the World Cup, had helped end the far right's monopoly of the flag.

'It is encouraging that a recent Mori poll demonstrated that 86% of people disagreed that you have to be white to be British,' said Mr Blunkett. 'Compare this with the overt racism of 40 years ago and there is hope and optimism for the future. Equally the reclaiming of the flag . . . must be sustained if we are to see off the BNP and the National Front in their efforts to foster fear, mistrust, and exploit concerns which emerge at a time of change.'

The home secretary's comments last night are likely to come under fire from critics who associate the flag of St George more with racist hooligans and those who argue that 'there ain't no black in the union jack' rather than with a symbol that can be embraced by black Britons. His speech came as the Home Office published figures showing that by March last year 17.5% of staff working in the immigration service came from minority ethnic groups; in the passport service the staffing figure was 12.7%; in the probation service 9.8%; in the prison service 3.7%; and in the police service 3.1%.

Mr Blunkett also announced his intention to set up a race equality advisory panel of up to 12 people to advise ministers and civil servants. The high level steering group of the Stephen Lawrence inquiry, now entering the third year of its work, is to switch focus to look at issues including training and development, racist incidents, and 'stop and search' by the police.

© Guardian Newspapers Limited 2002

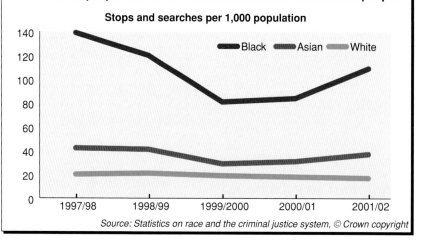

Stops and searches

Compared with 1999/2000, the number of recorded stops and searches fell by 14% for white people but rose by 6% for black people and 3% for Asians in the Metropolitan Police Area (MPS). In England and Wales (excluding the MPS) the falls were greater with an average fall of about 18% for white people and 6% for Asians but a rise of 4% for black people.

Stops and searches per 1,000 population

Black — Asian — White

Source: Statistics on race and the criminal justice system, © Crown copyright

Fighting racism

What the YRE is

Youth against Racism in Europe (YRE) is a campaigning international youth organisation, active in different countries across Europe. YRE was launched by an international demonstration of 40,000 people against racism in Brussels, in October 1992.

We keep in touch regularly with each other about what is happening in different countries and how we can build international campaigns against racism. In August 1994 we organised an anti-racist camp of 1,500 young people from all over Europe in Germany.

YRE believes that racism isn't natural; it is something that people learn and can be overcome through education and campaigning. Unemployment, homelessness and poverty can all be used to encourage racism by Nazis and politicians. Black and Asian people are a visible minority in European countries, and therefore can easily be used as a scapegoat for social and economic problems.

YRE therefore don't just say racism is wrong but use economic arguments to convince people that blacks and Asians are not to blame for these problems. We think that the economic system we live in creates poverty, unemployment and low wages because it is run to make profits for the rich and powerful. We campaign for the right to a job, a home and an education for all and

Young people of all races, Asian, Black and white, must unite against racism. We are the ones who have most to lose from racism and the neo-Nazi movement, and most to gain from their defeat

show that we can fight for these things best by overcoming racism and uniting.

YRE also campaigns to drive neo-Nazi groups – like the British National Party (BNP) and the National Front (NF) – out of our communities. Wherever they organise we will mobilise local people to oppose them – in order to prevent them from spreading their Nazi ideas and recruiting new members. The YRE was part of the successful campaign to close the British National Party's Headquarters in South-East London. We co-organised the two biggest national demonstrations of 8,000 and 50,000 which eventually succeeded in shutting it.

We were an important part of the successful campaign to defeat the BNP in Tower Hamlets, East London, in the mid-1990s. More recently YRE members have been actively campaigning against the BNP in areas like Lancashire, Yorkshire and Staffordshire.

We are campaigning for justice for people who have been unjustly imprisoned like Oliver Campbell, Winston Silcott and Satpal Ram, who YRE believes are the victims of racist frame-ups. We support campaigns for justice for the victims of racist attacks, and victims of police racism and brutality.

We campaign to defend refugees' right to asylum: against racist immigration laws, and the imprisonment of asylum-seekers. YRE takes up individual cases of people threatened with deportation and exposes the wider injustice of the present immigration system. We campaign to answer the myths and prejudices that have been spread against asylum-seekers by newspapers, the TV and radio, as well as the government and politicians.

We encourage local communities and asylum-seekers to work together to campaign for more resources for public services like schools, hospitals, doctors and

housing. But we also campaign against the dictatorships, repression and wars that force refugees to leave their homes. YRE believes that the only way to end the refugee crisis is to campaign internationally to put an end to the injustice, poverty and exploitation that exists around the world.

YRE members are against all forms of discrimination. We believe everyone should have equal rights whether they are Asian, Black or white, male or female, disabled or able-bodied, Muslim or non-Muslim, Jewish or gentile, atheist or religious.

School student members of YRE are active in combating racism both inside and outside school. We regularly visit schools to speak with the students about racism and fascism and what can be done about them. YRE has members in different schools, in estates, towns, cities and universities.

YRE is run and controlled by its members. We also work with a number of other groups – from local community groups to national organisations and trade unions.

Young people of all races, Asian, Black and white, must unite against racism. We are the ones who have most to lose from racism and the neo-Nazi movement, and most to gain from their defeat. United we can win!

■ For more information on the work of Youth against Racism in Europe (YRE), visit their web site at www.yre.org.uk

©Youth against Racism in Europe (YRE)

KEY FACTS

- Racism takes many different forms. These can include:
  - Personal attacks of any kind, including violence
  - Written or verbal threats or insults
  - Damage to property, including graffiti. (p. 1)

- Racist incidents ranging from harassment and abuse to physical violence are offences under the criminal law. Inciting racial hatred is also a criminal offence. (p. 1)

- A recent MORI poll found that people estimated that ethnic minorities comprised 22.5% of the total population, nearly three times the actual size. (p. 3)

- 9.9% of the population in England and Wales in April 2001 identified themselves as being from an ethnic minority (including 1.2% Irish). 87.5% gave their origin as White British. (p. 3)

- London is the region with the highest proportion of people from an ethnic minority (32.1%). (p. 3)

- Prejudice is prejudging people in a negative way according to preconceived ideas about them. (p. 4)

- More than half of the British population believe they live in a racist society, according to a major survey on race relations. (p. 5)

- Of all those questioned, 51% said they felt Britain is a racist society. That view was shared by 52% of whites and 53% of blacks. (p. 5)

- 2 in 3 women think race can limit either a person's choice of career or career progression. (p. 8)

- Whilst 86% of the British public disagree that to be truly British you have to be white, there is no consistent view on what it means to be British. (p. 10)

- According to government figures for 2000/01, Black Caribbean and Black Other pupils were three times more likely than white ones to be permanently excluded from school. (p. 11)

- 71% of minority ethnic 16- to 19-year-olds are in full-time education compared with 58% of whites of the same age. (p. 11)

- In 2000-2001, police recorded 25,100 racially aggravated offences of which 12,455 incidents were of racially aggravated harassment. (p. 13)

- In 1999, the risk of being the victim of a racially motivated incident was considerably higher for members of minority ethnic groups than for White people. (p. 14)

- The estimated number of racially motivated offences in England and Wales fell from 390,000 in 1995 to 280,000 in 1999. (p. 14)

- Racially motivated incidents represented 12% of all crime against minority ethnic people compared with 2% for White people. (p. 14)

- In 2001/02 of 714,000 stops and searches recorded by the police, 12% were of black people (1.8% of the population). (p. 17)

- Almost a quarter of Britain's jail population of 72,416 people come from an ethnic minority background. (p. 18)

- Only Indian men come anywhere near the average weekly earnings of white men with a negative differential of £5. (p. 20)

- Mosques have been attacked, people get threats over the phone, abuse gets shouted at children, not because they are Asian but because they are Muslims. (p. 21)

- At the moment discriminating against someone because they are a Muslim is not against the law. (p. 24)

- In London compared with the previous year, the number of stop and searches rose by eight per cent for white people, 30 per cent for black people and 40 per cent for Asians. (p. 33)

- A recent Mori poll demonstrated that 86% of people disagreed that you have to be white to be British. (p. 38)

You might like to contact the following organisations for further information. Due to the increasing cost of postage, many organisations cannot respond to enquiries unless they receive a stamped, addressed envelope.

Black Information Link – The 1990 Trust
Room 12, Winchester House
9 Cranmer Road
London, SW9 6EJ
Tel: 020 7582 1990
0870 127 7657
E-mail: blink1990@blink.org.uk
Web site: www.blink.org.uk
The main communication channel of The 1990 Trust. Its vision is the elimination of racial discrimination, the realisation of human rights for all.

ChildLine
2nd Floor Royal Mail Building
50 Studd Street
London, N1 0QW
Tel: 020 7239 1000
Fax: 020 7239 1001
E-mail: reception@childline.org.uk
Web site: www.childline.org.uk
A free, national helpline for children and young people in trouble or danger. Provides confidential phone counselling service for any child with any problem 24 hours a day. Children or young people can phone or write free of charge about problems of any kind to: ChildLine, Freepost 1111, London N1 0BR. Tel: Freephone 0800 1111.

Commission for Racial Equality (CRE)
St Dunstan's House
201-211 Borough High Street
London, SE1 1GZ
Tel: 020 7939 0000
Fax: 020 7931 0429
E-mail: info@cre.gov.uk
Web site: www.cre.gov.uk
Works for racial equality, for a just society, which gives everyone an equal chance to work, learn and live free from discrimination and prejudice, and from a fear of racial harassment and violence.

European Monitoring Centre on Racism and Xenophobia (EUMC)
Rahlgasse 3
A – 1060 Vienna, Austria
Tel: + 43 1 580 3000
Fax: + 43 1 580 3099
E-mail: information@eumc.eu.int
Web site: eumc.eu.int
Provides the Community and its Member States with objective, reliable and comparable information and data on racism, xenophobia, Islamophobia and anti-Semitism.

Institute of Race Relations (IRR)
2-6 Leeke Street
London, WC1X 9HS
Tel: 020 7837 0041
Fax: 020 7278 0623
E-mail: info@irr.org.uk
Web site: www.irr.org.uk
The Institute of Race Relations was established as an independent educational charity in 1958 to carry out research, publish and collect resources on race relations throughout the world.

Jewish Council for Racial Equality
33 Seymour Place
London, W1H 6AT
Tel: 020 8455 0896
Fax: 020 8458 4700
E-mail: j.core@btconnect.com
Web site: www.jcore.org.uk
JCORE works on three fronts: race equality education, Black-Jewish dialogue and asylum and refugee issues. Works within the community to raise awareness of racism and to encourage active involvement in building a just multicultural society.

Minority Rights Group International
379 Brixton Road
London, SW9 7DE
Tel: 020 7978 9498
Fax: 020 7738 6265
E-mail: minorityrights@mrgmail.org
Web site: www.minorityrights.org
Works to secure the rights of ethnic, religious and linguistic minorities and indigenous peoples worldwide, and to promote cooperation and understanding between communities.

The Monitoring Group
14 Featherstone Road
Southall,
Middlesex, UB2 5AA
Tel: 020 8843 2333
Fax: 020 8813 9734
E-mail: admin@monitoring-group.co.uk
Web site: www.monitoring-group.co.uk
The Monitoring Group provides a range of services for victims of racial harassment and domestic violence.

Race for Racial Justice
PO Box 1129
Croydon, CR9 1BD
Tel: 020 7273 3881
Fax: 079 49 116806
E-mail: racialjustice@btopenworld.com
Web site: www.racialjustice.org.uk
The Race for Racial Justice charity campaign aims to unite communities across Britain against racism.

Trades Union Congress – Equal Rights Department (TUC)
Congress House
23-28 Great Russell Street
London, WC1B 3LS
Tel: 020 7636 4030
Fax: 020 7636 0632
E-mail: info@tuc.org.uk
Web site: www.tuc.org.uk
The TUC has over 75 member trade unions, representing nearly seven million people from all walks of life.

Youth against Racism in Europe (YRE)
PO Box 858
London, E11 1YG
Tel: 020 8558 7947
Fax: 020 8533 4533
E-mail: yrehq@yahoo.co.uk
Web site: www.yre.org.uk
Youth against Racism in Europe (YRE) is a campaigning international youth organisation, active in 16 countries in Europe.

INDEX

ACKNOWLEDGEMENTS

The publisher is grateful for permission to reproduce the following material.

While every care has been taken to trace and acknowledge copyright, the publisher tenders its apology for any accidental infringement or where copyright has proved untraceable. The publisher would be pleased to come to a suitable arrangement in any such case with the rightful owner.

Chapter One: Racial Discrimination

Racism, © ChildLine, *Multi-cultural United Kingdom*, © Race for Racial Justice, *Replacing myths with facts*, © Commission for Racial Equality, *Race definitions*, © Race for Racial Justice, *Risk of being a victm of racially motivated offences*, © Crown copyright is reproduced with the permission of Her Majesty's Stationery Office, *We live in a racist society, reveals ICM poll*, © Black Information Link/The 1990 Trust, *Minority ethnic groups in the UK*, © Crown copyright is reproduced with the permission of Her Majesty's Stationery Office, *Minority ethic groups*, © Crown copyright is reproduced with the permission of Her Majesty's Stationery Office, *Survey on race*, © Commision for Racial Equality/She Magazine, *Minorities accuse TV and radio of tokenism*, © Guardian Newspapers Limited 2002, *Race is no barrier to 'being British'*, © 2002 MORI, *Education*, © Institute of Race Relations, *Minority ethnic pupils in mainly white schools*, © Crown copyright is reproduced with the permission of Her Majesty's Stationery Office, *Racial violence*, © Institute of Race Relations, *Victims of racial crime*, © Crown copyright is reproduced with the permission of Her Majesty's Stationery Office, *Racially motivated incidents*, © Crown copyright is reproduced with the permission of Her Majesty's Stationery Office, *White victims of race hatred*, © The Daily Mail, February 2003, *The criminal justice system*, © Institute of Race Relations, *Inequality in justice*, © Guardian Newspapers Limited 2002, *Arrests*, © Crown copyright is reproduced with the permission of Her Majesty's Stationery Office, *We have police in our sights, says race watchdog*, © Guardian Newspapers Limited 2002, *Black and underpaid*, © Trades Union Congress, *Weekly earnings*, © Trades Union Congress, *Religious discrimination and harassment*, © Britkid, *Muslims in Britain*, © Minority Rights Group International, *Main populations of Muslims in Britain*, Adapted from The Guardian, 17 June 2002, Minority Rights Group International, *Islamaphobia*, © Britkid, *Islamabad thing*, © Exposure Magazine.

Chapter Two: Tackling Racism

Moving towards a just, multicultural Britain, © Jewish Council for Racial Equality, *Your rights*, © Commission for Racial Equality, *Racial harassment*, © The Monitoring Group, *You can do something*, © 2003 European Monitoring Centre on Racism and Xenophobia, *Race the future*, © Exposure Magazine, *New unit to 'root out police racism'*, © Telegraph Group Limited, London 2003, *A fair cop?*, © Guardian Newspapers Limited 2002, *New action by prosecutors to stamp out hate crimes*, © Crown copyright is reproduced with the permission of Her Majesty's Stationery Office, *Fly the flag against racism*, © Guardian Newspapers Limited 2002, *Fighting racism*, © Youth against Racism in Europe (YRE).

Photographs and illustrations:

Pages 1, 16, 26: Pumpkin House; pages 5, 10, 13, 21, 28, 30, 34, 37: Simon Kneebone; pages 15, 32, 36: Bev Aisbett.

Craig Donnellan
Cambridge
May, 2003